The Anger Management Workbook

for Women

A 5-Step Guide to Managing Your Emotions
and Breaking the Cycle of Anger

Julie Catalano, MSW, LICSW

ALTHEA
PRESS

The Anger Management Workbook *for* Women

For Neighborhood Counseling and Community Services, Inc.—committed to keeping community mental health services accessible to all, despite the odds.

Contents

Foreword

EVERY WOMAN will feel that she has found an empathic, listening ear and wise counselor in Julie Catalano while reading this helpful anger management workbook.

Enlivened by the stories of Beatrice, Bobbi, Brittany, Emily, Haniya, and Margaret, this workbook presents a variety of evidence-based tools for women who wish to handle their anger differently.

Anger is no longer a taboo topic for women, as it was when Harriet Lerner wrote her groundbreaking book, *The Dance of Anger*, in 1985. In fact, I have been pleased to observe the lessening of traditional gender-role socialization over the past 30 years. No longer are most growing girls taught to adhere to the old norm of stifling their anger to meet the perpetually pleasant, nurturing feminine ideal. Nevertheless, women in the twenty-first century continue to struggle to find effective ways to achieve equity in relationships and respectful treatment in the workplace. Disrespectful treatment produces anger—but women are disappointed in themselves when they have an angry outburst. They do not feel good about yelling, crying, and screaming. Equally problematic for many of us is a tendency to swallow the anger (an "inburst"), which leaves the grievance smoldering and unresolved. In my own research, women often used cooking metaphors, such as "simmering," "stewing," or "slow boil," to describe an undercurrent of unexpressed anger within their bodies. That suppressed anger can lead to migraines, gastric distress, and other painful physical manifestations.

I became a researcher of women's anger not long after reading Lerner's 1985 book, when I discovered a huge void in the literature. Research abounded on women's anxiety and depression, but my team's study was actually the first large investigation of the anger of ordinary women (reported in the book *Women and Anger*, 1993). We recruited women from diverse workplaces, educational settings, and community clubs across the United States. Beyond studying anger in American women, the project then expanded with new collaborators in France and Turkey. Women are not a monolithic group, and the norms of a woman's culture, social stratum, and community create some variability. But some commonalities among women were found, regardless of culture: Their anger stories were stories of hurt, distress, embarrassment, regret, and shame. Women seldom felt good about their anger behavior.

No longer are most growing girls taught to adhere to the old norm of stifling their anger to meet the perpetually pleasant, nurturing feminine ideal.

Our studies negated several prevalent societal myths. For example, you may have heard that women don't know when they are angry. I can assure you that we never encountered a woman who was unaware of her anger. You may also have heard that women's anger is irrational. Not true. Women's anger is legitimate. It is squarely grounded in interpersonal interactions in which other people deny women power or resources, treat them unjustly, or behave irresponsibly toward them. In short, women have good reasons to be angry. So what is the problem? Few women learn constructive techniques for managing anger and resolving conflicts. Some of us received critical or abusive treatment that silenced us for years. But anger behavior is learned, and therefore it can be changed. That is the gap this workbook seeks to fill.

Nothing is more rewarding to a researcher than to have her work used by others. Julie Catalano has drawn from our research, and that of others, to provide women with gentle encouragement; useful self-assessment quizzes; and practical, concrete strategies for building new anger management skills. She has refined these strategies over many years of conducting women's anger management groups. One of this book's strengths is the inclusion of anger scenarios in same-sex partnerships, often omitted in other workbooks.

The author also speaks directly to women who lack resources for financial stability, decent housing, and social support. Managing anger effectively is a concern for all women.

The FADE application used in this book accurately depicts what all women should aim for: *feeling* better about managing anger, *appearing* differently to others, *doing* things differently, and being *empowered* when managing anger better. Wisely, Julie reminds us that changing our behavior takes time. Women should also anticipate some pushback from coworkers and family members who may not like their new assertive and self-protective actions. Self-validation and self-care will be important when such pushback from other people is encountered. The book contains much valuable information on mindfulness, meditation, exercise, and other health-promoting, self-care activities. Practicing new anger behaviors with supportive friends or family members is essential before tackling tough workplace scenarios. Facing a tough scenario, whether in the workplace or an intimate relationship, requires acknowledgment of the possibility that the other person will simply deny reality and responsibility. As Julie suggests, it's all about practice, practice, practice.

I like the metaphor of the white light, used by some feminist therapists to depict anger as a clear, strong emotion that provides energy to act on one's own behalf. The white light of anger can produce a new sense of self, with the right to verbalize genuine feelings and set limits on others who trample on this right. Anger can be a catalyst for courageous action.

I wish you well in your personal journey toward empowerment.

SANDRA P. THOMAS, PHD, RN, FAAN
Editor, Issues in Mental Health Nursing
Sara and Ross Croley Endowed Professor in Nursing
University of Tennessee, Knoxville

Introduction

IT'S QUIET in the office waiting room as new members of the women's anger management group continue to file in. Many women, such as these, often feel alone and ashamed of their angry feelings and behaviors. Coming in for help is a big step. Burdened by societal, cultural, ethnic, or religious pressures, women tend to behave "properly" in the ways proscribed for them. They often suppress or ignore anger in order to keep jobs, families, and relationships together. Women who don't stay within those confines and instead act out in anger often feel shame and remorse.

Women seek anger management for a variety of reasons. Some are here due to legal issues, such as court-mandated treatment, or referrals through social services. Others are here because of an employee assistance program (EAP).

Emily was mandated by a probate judge to seek treatment. After she was denied unsupervised visits with her children, she went to the family home, pounded on the door, and demanded to see her children. The incident ended with Emily taken away in handcuffs and a restraining order filed against her by her ex-husband. Learning to better manage her anger will be a crucial part of whether Emily gets to see her children again.

Haniya came to the group through her job's EAP. She is frequently aggravated by coworkers and often chastises them, because their "lazy incompetence" creates more work for her. What Haniya learns from this group about managing her anger may determine whether she can keep her dream job at a well-known tech company.

In Margaret's case, she was convinced to seek help by an elder-services worker. She is the caregiver of her elderly partner, who has dementia. Margaret finds it increasingly difficult to manage her temper as her partner's symptoms worsen. She feels terrible about her behavior, but as a self-described "lifelong loud and proud hothead," Margaret wonders if she can make the necessary changes to better care for both her partner and herself.

Some women self-refer to anger management to learn how to relate less angrily and more effectively with the closest people in their lives: intimate partners, children and other family members, friends, and coworkers. They are sad and frustrated about how their expressions of anger hurt their closest relationships.

Consider Beatrice. She feels unheard in her relationship, and she's angry about it. Usually Beatrice just tries to suppress her anger. But lately she's found herself feeling physically ill and suspects it has something to do with the rage she silently carries around.

Bobbi, a young, single mom with a six-year-old daughter, finds herself coming home from work filled with irritation and anger—admittedly over "stupid stuff." She tends to yell and swear at her daughter over insignificant things only to feel intense remorse and shame.

> A woman's decision to make changes about how she manages and expresses her anger often comes after a long and confusing struggle to right the wrongs in her life.

Brittany, a married mother of two children and a full-time manager in a medical billing office, fights with her husband "endlessly" over childcare and household chores. "He seems to think 'house elves' are going to appear from nowhere and do everything!" she says bitterly.

The women I've described all resemble patients I've treated during my more than 20 years as a clinical social worker in the Greater Boston area, working in the field of psychotherapy. I have the privilege of facilitating the women's anger management group in affiliation with Joseph Pereira, MSW, LICSW, of Outlook Associates, a private consulting firm that provides workshops and consultations for individuals and businesses on anger management. Joe has worked in this field for more than 30 years and runs the men's anger management groups.

A woman's decision to make changes about how she manages and expresses her anger often comes after a long and confusing struggle to right the wrongs in her life. Time and again, she ends up dismayed and ashamed when her angry outbursts result not in the changes she sought but, rather, in damaged relationships. This can occur at home, at work, or in her social network. Most women who seek anger treatment express terrible shame and remorse over negative expressions of anger—especially with loved ones. They lose self-respect and credibility during these episodes. When that occurs, women often feel resigned to stay quiet and quash their feelings in order to keep the peace within important relationships or systems of relationships, such as in a work environment or a family.

If you're at a place where your anger is wreaking havoc in your life, please know that you're not alone. By opening this book, you've taken an enormous step toward better managing your anger and fulfilling more of your needs and wants by acknowledging that there is a problem. It's my goal to give you the tools and resources you need to take control of your anger.

1 Approaching Anger

IN THIS CHAPTER, we will explore why women's experience of anger may be unique, how anger occurs in our brains and bodies, and—for better or for worse—the different ways we manifest it. We will learn why fueling anger with *more* angry thoughts and actions might feel good temporarily but doesn't truly serve our emotional needs. And finally, we will explore how to apply some of the ideas and skills from Cognitive Behavioral Therapy (CBT) and mindfulness to reduce the sting of anger.

The American Psychological Association defines *anger* as "an emotion characterized by antagonism toward someone or something you feel has deliberately done you wrong. Anger can be a good thing. It can give you a way to express negative feelings, for example, or motivate you to find solutions to problems." Anger is considered one of the "disruptive" emotions, but it's also as normal and natural as any other feeling.

Anger: Positives and Negatives

Anger is an emotion, and like any emotion, it is rooted in a natural human instinct— to protect, to survive, to stay safe. Although anger has accrued a largely negative connotation (especially for women), this emotion has both good and bad attributes. Let's review some of them here.

THE POSITIVES

We almost never consider the positive aspects of anger, but this emotion does have some benefits. It's often what we *do* with our anger that makes it so destructive—the feeling itself is just a feeling.

Anger is rooted in the body's "fight-or-flight" mechanism. This is when our brain sounds the alarm that we're in some kind of imminent physical danger, mobilizing us to run away or stand and fight. This mechanism has helped humans survive for millions of years. (We will talk in more detail about the fight-or-flight mechanism further on in this chapter.)

Anger is an energizing emotion. It propels a neurochemical chain reaction that helps us take action. In contrast to the category of the submissive emotions (e.g., depression, anxiety, embarrassment), which have an effect of lowering our available energy, anger gives us an energetic jolt. Channeled properly, this energy can help us make needed changes.

Anger lets us know that we have experienced a violation. It's how we know that something isn't right and needs our attention. Simmering, sullen anger or ongoing outbursts with a particular person in our lives can be a sign that our needs are not being met in the relationship. Too much is being asked of us, or we are being emotionally hurt in some way. Single moments of outrage at the behavior of an acquaintance or stranger can let us know not to get further involved with that person.

Expressed anger lets others know that they have violated a boundary and that they should stop. Once we are aware that we're experiencing a singular or ongoing violation, anger gives us the energy and focus to express our wants and needs and to request change from others.

 We can always learn new ways to respond to anger. Anger responses are learned behaviors, not instinctive. This makes it much easier for us to manage those responses, rather than trying to control our body's physiological reactions to anger triggers. This means, it's easier to change our *outward* anger behaviors than to change the *internal* experience of anger. This extremely important step helps repair damaged relationships and stops the repetitive cycle of acting out followed by remorse, shame, and guilt. We act differently, so we begin to feel different.

THE NEGATIVES

Conversely, it's more common to associate anger with the negative outward responses that can wreak havoc on our relationships and lives. Those outcomes become synonymous with the feeling itself. Let's explore them while keeping in mind that the negative outcomes described below are *behaviors* associated with anger, not the emotion itself.

Long-term untreated anger has been proven to lead to cardiovascular disease and is suspected in other diseases. Beatrice and Margaret are two sides of the same health-risk coin. Beatrice continually internalizes her anger, which results in headaches and neck, back, and stomach pain. She may get treatment for the symptoms, but the root of the problem—her unexpressed anger—won't go away. Margaret habitually externalizes her anger by yelling and cursing. Her outbursts have caused her blood pressure to rise, and she's now taking medication to lower it.

Venting anger at others keeps the flames going and makes others feel attacked. Emily talks to her best friend about her arrest and her ex-husband. But rather than having a two-way conversation, she talks *at* her friend. Emily tends to retell incidents with the same level of anger with which she experienced them—with a raised voice, foul language, and tense body language. Emily isn't angry with her friend; she is only venting. But her friend feels uncomfortable and triggered by the level of anger Emily expresses in that moment. These venting sessions don't help Emily deescalate these feelings and get the relief she is looking for. Instead, they only help maintain her same level of anger arousal.

Outward expressions of anger toward other people or property (e.g., throwing things, yelling, name-calling, hitting) **are considered to be acts of aggression.** These outbursts are scary to those around us who become uncomfortable at best and afraid for their safety at worst. Haniya, for example, tends to yell at coworkers and call them names. This behavior has resulted in their being afraid to interact with her, and rather than address the issue with her directly, they report her actions to the human resources (HR) department.

Unchecked outward expressions of anger cause us to look unhinged, or out of control, to those around us. Even if you know you're right or justified, these outbursts cause you to lose credibility. Emily's decision to go to the family home and demand to see her children, despite a court order that she couldn't be there, resulted in her arrest. When Margaret yells at her partner, Jane—who has dementia—and tries to physically force her to do things, it makes Jane angry; in turn she becomes afraid and uncooperative.

Inward, simmering anger fuels resentments and creates distance in important relationships. Think about smoke rising out of a volcano—it's pretty clear that something's brewing inside, right? Beatrice has an ever-growing list of transgressions committed against her by her wife, Sarah. However, Sarah doesn't directly know about any of them. She does, however, feel the steely coldness that Beatrice projects at times. Even other people in their lives sense anger from Beatrice. But when Sarah asks what's wrong, Beatrice replies that nothing is wrong, she's fine.

Treating people with overt anger will result in their treating us with overt or covert anger in return. Accusatory behavior, such as blaming language, pointing, yelling, or name-calling, will generally cause the other person's anger to become aroused, and they will respond in a defensive manner. Depending on the balance of power in the relationship, the person likely will come back at us directly, or retaliate in some other (less direct) way, such as gossiping behind our backs.

Modeling out-of-control anger behavior for children teaches them to manage their own anger that way. Bobbi grew up witnessing her parents' ongoing displays of distress. She endured their bouts of yelling, hitting, and saying intentionally hurtful things to each other and to her and her siblings. Bobbi also knows that she is unintentionally acting the same way at times with her daughter, Shania.

It's Not the Emotion; It's the Response

Let's take a closer look at anger's physiological origins within our bodies. How do we learn to respond to anger in the ways we do? How can internalizing anger, and expressing it explosively, damage our health? We will learn how anger and aggression are two different things; one can be angry, and express anger, without becoming aggressive.

I mentioned Haniya in the introduction. At the start of group, she sits with her arms folded over her chest and her legs crossed. Her face is tense, while her jaw continuously locks and unlocks. During introductions, she talks about how, as a project manager, she works day and night to meet deadlines despite being dragged down by the "incompetence of the imbeciles" she works with. And now she *is the one being threatened with a performance improvement plan at work? How can this be?*

The purpose of anger management isn't to become a saint or to no longer experience angry feelings at all. Anger is an emotion that holds an important role in your psychological and emotional life. It helps you know when you need to make changes and adjustments to situations around you. In fact, researchers assert that people seek therapy for anger almost as much as for anxiety, the number one reason for seeking therapy. The objective is to figure out when, how, and with whom you can effectively express anger in order to better achieve your goals.

If you're similar to Haniya, you're prone to expressing anger outwardly in a way that causes you a lot of internal suffering. Like her, you may experience a buildup of negative thoughts about coworkers or other people in your life. This may fuel your justification for angrily acting out when something finally pushes you over the edge; one last negative thought, one last interpretation of someone's behavior, and you explode. Your reaction may cause you to pound on your desk, throw something, or use vulgar language toward someone. You may feel momentary relief, but soon after, you begin to feel embarrassed, remorseful, and ashamed, and find yourself apologizing. Eventually the cycle will begin again.

Some people don't experience much outward anger at work, but once they get home, they explode. Perhaps you find yourself taking out your daily stress on those closest to you, as in the case of Bobbi. The single mother finds herself yelling and swearing at her young daughter. Or maybe you bottle up your anger, as Beatrice does, trying to deny it, but then become physically ill.

Aggression and anger are two different things. Anger is simply the emotion you feel when conditions around you conflict with how you want them to be. Aggression is your outward expression of anger in a way that is harmful to other people, property, or yourself. Aggression doesn't help solve anything. Instead, it causes you, and those around you, to suffer. Responding to anger in this way is a learned behavior, usually stemming from how your family of origin handled the emotion of anger. Perhaps you've been abused, and your reaction to trauma causes you to angrily act out in ways that are painful.

Know that whatever way you've learned to act out when angry, you can learn new behaviors that cause you—and those important to you—a lot less suffering.

Angry Brain, Angry Body

Anger is not a moral issue, although most major world religions prescribe that their followers contain their anger; to not act out aggressively is deemed virtuous. Anger management is mentioned in several well-known quotes attributed to Siddhartha Gautama, or Buddha (following enlightenment). The Thirukkural, a 2,200-year-old text used by the Tamil people of India and Sri Lanka, contains advice on ethical behavior in many areas of life, including managing anger and angry reactions. It is organized in Adhikarams, groups of 10 couplets each on a particular subject. For example, couplet 129 in Adhikaram 13, "The Possession of Self-Restraint," says, "The wound made by hurting with fire will heal, but the wound created by harsh words uttered using our tongue leaves an indelible scar." In Adhikaram 31, on "Not Being Angry," the writer, Thiruvalluvar, a well-known poet and philosopher during this era, advises readers that anger can be harmful especially to the person who is angry. "If a man guard himself, let him guard himself against anger; if he does not guard it, anger will kill him" (couplet 305).

Anger is a normal, everyday emotion rooted firmly in the human brain for eons to help us survive as a species. The brain contains pieces from every stage of human evolutionary history, and some of these remain quite primitive. One of these more primitive parts is the *amygdala*, home to emotional memory and the fight-or-flight response. Remember, this is the body's alarm system, responsible for summoning the power and energy to fight or flee in response to immediate danger. The amygdala, located within the limbic system, receives data from the world around us. It

A WORD ABOUT SAFETY

No progress can be made in managing your anger if it's so out of control that people are being harmed. Any form of physical aggression toward another person must be stopped before this work can begin. If you feel that your anger has become too out of control and that you are in danger of harming someone in your care, **get help immediately.** Below are two numbers that may be of use. For a more complete listing of these resources, please consult the Resources section in the back of this book.

- The National Parent Helpline: available weekdays 10 a.m. to 7 p.m. PST at (855) 427-2736

- The Alzheimer's Association: a 24-hour helpline for caregivers at (800) 272-3900.

If a partner or a family member is abusing you or if you feel there may be mutual abuse occurring, get help right away. You can call the National Domestic Violence Hotline at (800) 799-SAFE (7233). For a more complete listing of these resources, please consult the Resources section at the back of this book.

When you are starting anger management work, there *must* be a baseline of physical safety for yourself and those around you. Once you've achieved that, you have already come a long way.

then either sends that information to the *prefrontal cortex*—the part of the brain responsible for thinking and judgment—or immediately sounds the fight-or-flight alarm, without taking time for judgment or thought. If the information received has enough emotional intensity, the amygdala will sound the alarm that immediate action is needed. These parts of our brain are responsible for our very survival. They're also involved in the physical experience of anger.

ANATOMY OF AN ANGER INCIDENT

You sleep through your alarm and wake up late for work. The body's sympathetic nervous system kicks in, with the amygdala sending out the alarm that there is a threat. This triggers the fight-or-flight state. The amygdala isn't sophisticated enough to calibrate the *level* of threat—just that there is one. It then sends the signal to flood the body with chemicals to tense muscles, raise the heart rate, and increase breathing. Your fight-or-flight response may *feel* like "This is a matter of life and death!" even though you are simply late for work. This is when the negative thinking begins: "I'm so screwed. You idiot! Why did you do this again?"

You jump out of bed and realize that you forgot you have an important meeting first thing in the morning. You feel panic as more chemicals, such as epinephrine and norepinephrine, are released into the body, followed by more physical sensations, followed by more exaggerated thoughts.

You get in your car and realize that you are almost out of gas. The amygdala continues to sound the threat alarm, and neurotransmitters and hormones, such as adrenaline and noradrenaline, continue to prime your body for fight. Cognitively, your attention narrows. It's difficult to think of anything other than the predicament you're in. Everything around you seems too slow—the gas station attendant, the traffic, the red lights. You shout in your car, "Come on, come on, I'm late!" Your thoughts begin to rationalize: "Idiot drivers getting in my way! Why do they have to make these meetings so early anyway? My boss is an idiot to keep scheduling these pointless meetings."

The driver in back of you is tailgating you. You keep looking in your rearview mirror, giving the other driver mean looks. More threat messages are sent from the amygdala, followed by the release of more fight-or-flight chemicals, followed by more angry thoughts: "I should stop short just to show this idiot. He thinks he can intimidate me—well, I'll kick his a**!"

The driver who was tailgating you now cuts directly in front of you, and you must hit the brakes—hard. Your brain and body are already seriously into fight-or-flight mode, but the amygdala sounds the alarm yet again to this new insult, and the brain is flooded with yet more neurotransmitters; the body fills with more hormones, your muscles tense, your heart pumps, and your breathing gets harder.

You pound the steering wheel as hard as you can, cursing and yelling. With your heart pounding, adrenaline flowing, and rapid breathing, you can't think of anything at all except this horrible situation. You think, "I can't take this anymore—I hate my life!" But after a minute or so of yelling and pounding the steering wheel, you begin to feel spent. Your breath starts to slow, your heart rate slowly returns to normal, and you start to think more clearly. "I'd better pull myself together; I'm almost at work." Your body expends the built-up hormones and other chemicals, and the amygdala stops sounding the alarm. That's when your body's parasympathetic nervous system kicks in to begin sending calming chemicals and messages to slow your heart rate, breathing, and perspiration.

You park and slowly get out of your car, realizing that your shirt is covered in sweat and your hand is sore from pounding the steering wheel. At your desk, you check your e-mail only to find the meeting is canceled because your boss is out sick. You think back to the scene in your car and start to feel embarrassed. You can remember feeling furious but find it difficult to call up the feeling now. "I really have to learn how to get a grip on myself," you think, sheepishly.

As you can see, anger can easily arise out of life's everyday stressors. If we aren't able to engage our brain's prefrontal cortex early on—the part of the brain responsible for reasoning and decision-making—when these stressors arise, the body's sympathetic nervous system can become activated as if under serious threat. Once we are triggered, it becomes more difficult to remain open to reason. It can take anywhere from 30 minutes to more than an hour for the body to reabsorb all of the fight-or-flight chemicals once they are released.

The physiological experience of anger is instinctive. In order to make wise choices about your behavior once your anger has become aroused, you must learn to engage the part of your brain that lets you think and make decisions, the prefrontal cortex. The techniques described in this book will help you do just that.

Your responses to anger are learned. In order to change them, you must learn new responses, although it's no easy task. See pages 8 and 9 for an example from everyday life that illustrates what happens in the brain and body once anger is aroused.

Anger across Gender Lines

The actual physiological experience of anger appears to be the same for women as it is for men. Anger is anger, in other words. However, the triggers, targets, expressions, and, perhaps most important, the *consequences* of that expression are different for women. In the United States, it's socially acceptable for men to become angry more often and to show anger more easily. This may be because anger is associated with power and status. However, while it is generally more socially and culturally acceptable for men to express anger than women, it is in fact women who are more vocal about their anger and seem to hold on to it longer. The 1995 Aging and the Sense of Control survey, conducted by John Mirowsky and Catherine Ross of the University of Texas, surveyed 2,592 US adults ages 18 to 95. It found that women are more likely than men to express their anger by yelling. The 1996 General Social Survey, conducted by the National Opinion Research Center, found in a sample of 1,460 adults that women also ruminate more on their anger, talk more with the people who are the targets of their anger, and take longer to cool down.

Between 1989 and 1997, the Women's Anger Project studied the everyday anger of approximately 700 women in the United States, Turkey, and France. The two-phase study was conducted by Dr. Sandra Thomas and her colleagues at the University of Tennessee, University of North Carolina, and Emory University and looked at the effect of racism and oppression on stress and anger levels in women's lives. In general, the higher the socioeconomic level someone held, the more she was allowed to express anger.

ANGER SELF-ASSESSMENT

The following anger self-assessment is meant to uncover the severity and frequency of your anger responses. This is not a formal diagnostic tool, but rather it is for informational purposes to help give some direction to your anger management work.

Please respond to the following statements and add up your total score. Circle 1 for *never*, 2 for *rarely*, 3 for *sometimes*, 4 for *frequently*, or 5 for *always*.

1. I often feel physical pain, such as stomachaches or headaches, when I am angry.
    1   2   3   4   5   *1*

2. I try to hide my anger from others.
    1   2   3   4   5   *3*

3. When I am angry at someone, I will gossip about that person or try to sabotage him or her in some other way.
    1   2   3   4   5   *3.5*

4. When I am angry, I take my frustration out on those closest to me, not the person with whom I am really angry.
    1   2   3   4   5   *4*

5. I am irritated by small things.
    1   2   3   4   5   *5*

6. I have a short fuse.
    1   2   3   4   5   *?3.5*

7. When I really feel angry, I want to hit someone.
    1   2   3   4   5   *1*

8. When I get really angry, I want to break things.
    1   2   3   4   5   *1*

9. I have obsessive thoughts that make me angry.
    1   2   3   4   5   *4*

→

26

10. It really irritates me when people don't understand what I am trying to tell them.

1   2   3   4   5   *4*

11. I blow my top at least once a week.

1   2   3   4   5   *4*

12. My anger outbursts upset the people around me.

1   2   3   4   5   *5*

13. I get really impatient when someone is driving too slowly in front of me.

1   2   3   4   5   *3*

14. I get angry when people break the rules, such as when they have too many items in the express checkout lane at the supermarket.

1   2   3   4   5   *3*

15. When people are rude around me, it makes me angry.

1   2   3   4   5   *4*

16. I find myself frequently irritated by specific people in my life.

1   2   3   4   5   *4*

17. I feel a lot of shame and guilt about my anger responses.

1   2   3   4   5   *5*

18. I often feel a lot of muscle tension and stress.

1   2   3   4   5   *3*

19. I yell or curse when I am angry.

1   2   3   4   5   *5*

20. I get so angry I feel like a volcano ready to explode.

1   2   3   4   5   *4*

21. I get frustrated quickly when machines or equipment don't work right.

1   2   3   4   5   *4.5*

48.5

22. I hang on to anger against people and situations for a long time.

1   2   3   4   5   3·5

23. I can't tolerate incompetent people. They make me angry.

1   2   3   4   5   4

24. I think people are trying to get away with things they shouldn't.

1   2   3   4   5   ~~5~~ 3

25. I have angry outbursts when family members don't do their share of the work at home.

1   2   3   4   5   2

TOTAL _____   12.5   61

Score Key:

80–100   Your anger expression is likely getting you into serious trouble with others. It would probably be worthwhile to seek professional help and to work through this book.

60–80   You may need professional help, but you certainly need to work on controlling your anger in a deliberate manner.

50–60   You have plenty of room for improvement. Reading self-help books on anger control could be beneficial.

30–50   You're probably getting angry as often as most people. Monitor your episodes of anger outbursts and see if you can lower your score in a few months.

Below 30   Good job. You are likely managing your anger well.

Adapted from Outlook Associates of New England Anger Assessment

It's well documented that men make more money than women, both on the whole and in specific fields. Men also hold more positions of authority in business and political life. The cultural pressure on women to be polite and quiet, coupled with men's hold on power and money in our culture and society, allows us to infer the reasons why it's more acceptable for men to openly express anger than it is for women.

But Thomas and her colleagues also discovered that women's anger is aroused by different circumstances than men's. One big difference is that women experience *vicarious stressors*; they are triggered not only by events and situations that directly affect them, but also by events that affect loved ones. So whatever upsets a spouse, parent, sibling, child, or friend also upsets the women connected to them.

Thomas said that the most common trigger for women's anger was powerlessness—women were trying to influence change in the workplace or with significant others but could not make that happen. Thomas found that women often reported that they felt as if significant others and coworkers didn't listen to their point of view.

The second most common trigger for women's anger was injustice. Many respondents in Thomas's studies gave examples of loved ones and coworkers treating them unfairly or with disrespect.

And finally, the third most common trigger for women's anger was "lack of responsibility." Women cited the shirking of responsibilities by intimate partners, children, and coworkers as being a big cause for anger.

Brittany's situation is one scenario that illustrates Thomas and her team's findings about differences in anger triggers across genders.

Brittany and her husband, Kyle, have been married for eight years and have two children, a seven-year-old boy in second grade and a three-year-old girl who attends preschool. Brittany works full-time, Monday through Friday, as a manager in a busy medical billing office, and Kyle is self-employed as an electrician, with jobs of varying sizes in progress at all times in different parts of the state. Brittany and Kyle wake up at 5 a.m. each day—he gets ready to leave for work, and she makes lunches for everybody, wakes the children, gets them dressed and fed, and drops them off at their separate schools, before finally arriving at work herself.

Kyle often gets out of work earlier and tries to go home for a quick nap before the family gets home, as his work is "more physically exhausting" than office work (he feels) and he needs a break. At 5 o'clock, Brittany leaves her job, quickly picks up her son from his after-school program, then dashes to pick up her daughter at preschool before it closes at 5:30—the school charges $1 for every minute that she's late.

Brittany has talked with Kyle many times about ways they might take turns with pickups and drop-offs, but Kyle insists that it will not work with the schedule maintained by most construction sites. She feels powerless to make any changes in the situation.

Brittany also feels she is treated unfairly by Kyle, as he "wanted to have kids just as much" as she did but doesn't see (or isn't willing to see) the amount of work required to care for them. She also feels that he shirks responsibility for helping manage the household, as he goes golfing on the weekend "to relieve stress," thus avoiding the weekend house-cleaning, laundry, food shopping, and so on.

Her anger builds and builds. She thinks about divorcing Kyle, as she feels she is "practically a single mom" anyway. She finds herself yelling at Kyle—and the kids—as her frustration rises and she doesn't see another way out of the situation. Yet she knows that she loves Kyle, they still sometimes have good times together, and her kids love their dad. Also, they need Kyle's income to maintain the household—it would be very hard on everyone if they split up. Brittany feels trapped.

Women respondents were found to be more open than men to the *anger discuss* method of handling anger. Anger discuss, a research term derived from the Framingham Anger Scales, involves talking about your anger at an emotionally safe time and place. Thomas elaborates on the method in the book *Women and Anger*.

This is by far the healthiest physical and emotional pathway when it comes to expressing your anger. We will explore the anger discuss method in much more detail later in the book.

Anger Exploration Journal

Let's now look at *your* daily experience of anger. It's important to find out as much information as you can about your experiences with anger. Put on your lab coat and get out your notebook, and prepare to collect as much data as possible regarding your anger outbursts or "inbursts." The best way to describe an inburst is when anger arousal occurs and you feel the physical symptoms of the fight-or-flight system kicking in—rapid heart rate, muscle tension, shallow breathing, perspiration. You will probably also experience the distorted thinking and rationalizations that justify your anger response. But instead of outwardly expressing your anger, you internalize it. You may feel as though you could explode, but you keep the anger inside. Following the prompts below, examine your most recent significant anger event with a fine-toothed comb. This will help put together a timeline for further study of your physical sensations, your thoughts, your behaviors, and ultimately, the outcomes.

Trigger event:

_____

Three Ws of the event (whom you were with, when it happened, what happened):

_____

_____

_____

How intense was your anger on a 1 to 10 scale (10 being completely infuriated)? _____

What physical sensations did you feel (e.g., increased heart rate, perspiration, trembling, faster breathing)?

_____

_____

_____

What negative thoughts fueled your anger (e.g., my child is purposely trying to drive me crazy, the driver of that car is ruining my day)?

_____

_____

_____

What were your physical expressions of anger (e.g., crossing arms, pointing, yelling, swearing, throwing something)?

_____

_____

_____

What was the outcome of this situation (positive, negative, neutral)?

_____

_____

Where do you think you could have done something differently?

_____

_____

_____

Adapted from Outlook Associates of New England Anger Log

You'll find more blank copies of this anger log at the end of the book and online at www.NeighborhoodCounselingServices.org. Try tracking your anger events for the next month or so. Do they happen with the same people or person? What time of day do they occur? Are there any precipitating events that trigger them? As you progress through this book, you will learn how to make sense of these patterns and change your reaction when you do get angry. I recommend keeping a journal handy for writing any new thoughts or feelings you experience.

What's Really Happening when We Experience Anger

When we experience anger, we are usually not being threatened to the point that we must physically fight. For example, if you're waiting in line at the supermarket or the bank and become irritable because the cashier is moving slowly, nothing is actually being done to you. However, your parasympathetic nervous system doesn't know that, and it creates an outsize response to the "threat."

Some people are more prone to anger responses than others. You probably know someone who is happy-go-lucky and doesn't seem bothered by much. That person may be blessed with a physiology that is slow to anger arousal. Perhaps she grew up in a family where she witnessed adults reacting to life stressors with less irritability and anger. Maybe she has a happy combination of both.

Other people may seem to appear to be in a state of constant anger. This personality characteristic is known as *trait anger*. Those who score higher on trait anger characteristics tend to maintain a baseline that is more prone to anger and irritability. Essentially, people with trait anger have shorter fuses. They view daily stressors through a lens of irritation. A person with a higher level of trait anger experiences anger more frequently and more intensely than others. Genetics may play a role, but researchers also see socialization—how a person is taught to express anger by important people in his or her environment—as another contributing factor.

People who suffer from post-traumatic stress disorder (PTSD) often experience emotional responses that are disproportionate to the level of the anger trigger. PTSD is a syndrome caused by traumatic events in a person's life, the symptoms of which can include increased anger and irritability. The disorder causes the parasympathetic nervous system to become hypervigilant and overly responsive to everyday-life triggers. This can cause people to become more easily irritated and volatile. PTSD and its role in anger are especially relevant to women, who are twice as likely to be diagnosed with PTSD as men.

Treating Anger

Various therapeutic approaches help with anger management. In this book I focus on two of them: CBT strategies and mindfulness. Armed with these tactics, you can effectively make positive changes in anger-related behavior and create self-care habits that make it less likely for seeds of anger to grow and develop into full-blown incidents.

COGNITIVE BEHAVIORAL THERAPY

If you're unfamiliar with CBT, it's a long-standing, well-studied psychotherapeutic technique with well-documented success. This technique is used to examine distorted or negative thoughts and their role in shaping undesirable behaviors, feelings, and outcomes. In addition to examining negative cognitions, or thoughts, and their role in fueling anger, you will also observe the body's response to anger. Often clients are surprised to notice the sheer number of sensations that arise within their bodies before an anger episode. Some of these responses are subtle; one client described a "rising" sense in her body just before an angry outburst. Other responses are more obvious, like a pounding heart rate, shallow breathing, or perspiration. Honoring what our bodies tell us, even before these sensations become thoughts, is an important step to managing anger better.

ALTHOUGH CBT AND SOME OF THE OTHER TECHNIQUES discussed in this book are best practiced in tandem with a trained therapist, this book illustrates certain methods that you can practice on your own. However, these methods are not intended as a replacement for psychotherapy. Please seek the help of a licensed professional when needed.

MINDFULNESS

In addition to CBT and monitoring physiological responses, you will also learn to employ mindfulness techniques to help reduce angry reactions. Mindfulness helps you awaken to the present moment that you're living, with your full physical and mental awareness of that moment. Mindfulness techniques help you focus your mind on one thing at a time, to be fully present. We will describe and practice mindfulness techniques more thoroughly throughout this book.

THE IMPORTANCE OF SELF-CARE

Finally, you will refine your self-care activities. We all pay lip service to good nutrition, adequate exercise, sufficient rest and sleep, and time with friends. In this book you'll practice integrating these soul-nourishing and anger-diffusing activities into your day. For anyone interested in lowering their anger reactivity, self-care activities are not an option—they're a must.

Positive Outcomes

This workbook outlines a five-step process. Using the AARM (assess, act, restore, maintain) steps, you'll start to learn new anger responses. Through the guided exercises, you will be able to do the following.

1. **Assess Your Anger.** Here, you'll monitor your body's physiological responses to anger, discovering the underlying thought patterns and rationalizations that contribute to your type of response. You'll also explore any additional feelings that accompany your anger and learn about your expression style, including the triggers and targets of your anger.

2. **Act.** You'll explore and utilize new approaches to better managing your anger. Techniques for managing physiological responses to triggers include changing the body's temperature, paced breathing, and intense exercise. You'll be introduced to "time-out" skills that encourage you to leave situations in which communication has broken down. You'll learn about "thought-stopping" techniques to stop your repetitive negative thoughts, reappraisal, distraction, how to express your feelings through art and music, mindfulness skills as a means to reduce reactivity, and how to choose better anger responses.

3. **Restore Communication (Part 1).** You'll lay the groundwork for more productive expression and discussion of your wants and needs by first assessing your conflict style. Essential communication skills, such as active listening and talking using "I" statements, will be introduced. In addition, you'll learn how to monitor your facial expressions and body language and how to pay attention to the underlying emotions in what the other person is communicating to you.

4. **Restore Communication (Part 2).** You'll learn and use techniques, such as Rosenberg's Four Steps of Nonviolent Communication and Gottman's four simple strategies, to improve communication of your wants and needs, as well as how to listen to the wants and needs of others.

5. **Maintain Progress.** You'll become equipped with the tools to implement new approaches to anger using self-care strategies, as well as ongoing self-awareness and behavioral monitoring.

Working through the exercises in this book will enable you to do the following:

- Recognize your body's physical signals that you are becoming angry.

- Recognize your brain's "go-to" choices of negative and unhelpful thoughts, which fuel anger reactions.

- Reflect upon your "learned" responses to anger triggers from your family of origin and how to change them.

- Identify what your triggers are.

- Identify who and what your targets are.

- Make conscious choices about how you respond to anger situations.

- Discern what conditions in your life contribute to your anger and how to change them.

- Practice effective communication techniques to express needs, wants, and requests.

- Practice mindfulness techniques to calm the mind and become open to the possibility of each moment.

- Plan and implement self-care in order to create more balance in your life.

FADE

Please take a moment to sit down and imagine how life will be when you're better able to manage your anger. Close your eyes or focus on a spot on the floor. Allow yourself to imagine a time, perhaps a few months from now, when you don't let your anger get the best of you. Record your experience below.

Feel (Imagine how you will feel both physically and emotionally if you were to manage anger better):

_____

_____

_____

Appear (Imagine how you may appear differently to others if you were to manage anger better):

_____

_____

_____

Do (Imagine what you would do differently if you were to manage anger better):

_____

_____

_____

Empower (Imagine what you would be empowered to do if you were to manage anger better):

_____

_____

_____

Make note of the ways in which you want your anger to **FADE** in the future. Hang on to these goals for future reference.

_____

_____

_____

_____

_____

_____

FIND NEW PROTECTION

Anger is a powerful and energizing emotion, one of the core instinctive human survival responses. For many of us, especially those who have been oppressed or abused, giving up the anger response is a frightening prospect. Perhaps these learned responses helped your grandmother or mother survive terrible situations in the past. Maybe angry outbursts have helped your ancestors get along and cope in life, up to a point. Anger responses can keep threatening people at bay and help set boundaries. But if you're seeking new ways to address what triggers your anger, then these responses have now outlived their purpose.

It's possible to set limits with other people, express your needs and wants, and attain more of your goals without angry outbursts or inbursts. You'll do this by learning more about the anger discuss mode of expressing anger, among other techniques. Many components go into an emotionally safe and productive conversation about what is irritating you. What's more, these discussions don't always begin with the person you're angry at. Applying the anger discuss method is more productive in the long run than lashing out, as it includes a listener who is sympathetic and interested in engaging in the discussion.

By using this book over the next 12 weeks or so, you can systematically evaluate your anger. What is your style of anger expression? What triggers your anger? What physiological responses do you experience when angry? Who and what are your targets? What thoughts fuel your anger, narrow your focus, and keep your anger going? You will try out new strategies for managing your body's responses to anger so that you can learn new behaviors in response to your physiological cues. Sometimes we begin to *act* better before we *feel* better. This is a wonderful place to start. You can't force your feelings to change, but they will change as you gain confidence in your ability to change your interactions for the better.

Chapter 1 Self-Evaluation

You'll be asked to check in at the end of each chapter so that you have a chance to process what you've learned and determine what information you'd like to keep with you going forward. In this chapter we learned about the positive and negative aspects of anger, how the body responds to anger, and how anger triggers and responses in women differ from those in men. We also previewed CBT and mindfulness as treatment approaches that we will use to manage anger in the coming chapters. Finally, we developed a vision of how or what we want to Feel, Appear, Do, and be Empowered once we make changes for the better in our anger responses. Please take a moment to write what stood out for you in chapter 1 and what you'd like to remember.

_____

_____

_____

_____

_____

_____

_____

_____

_____

_____

_____

2 Assessing Your Anger

During group, Margaret sits, holding her head in her hands. She feels helpless to change her behavioral responses since her anger "goes from 0 to 100 in no time flat." As a long-distance trucker, Margaret is used to being on her own, managing tough people and difficult situations. However, she is now on family medical leave, caring for her partner, Jane, whose Alzheimer's disease is worsening. Margaret loves Jane. But her partner's increasing forgetfulness, repetitive questioning, and agitation in the late afternoon, also known as "sundowning," are taking their toll. Margaret often finds herself screaming at Jane and slamming objects in the kitchen. She feels shame and remorse about her behavior.

Physiological Responses

To begin to better manage your anger, one of the first things you must tackle is understanding your body's physical reaction to an anger trigger. As we discussed in chapter 1, when you experience an anger trigger, the body's sympathetic nervous system goes into action, stimulating the instinctive fight-or-flight survival response. Before angry thoughts can form, even before you're fully aware of what is triggering you, your body is primed for action.

Below, you'll find a list of common physiological responses to anger. Think about your own anger incidents and try to recall their very beginnings. Assess your initial physiological anger responses. If you are like Margaret, this may take some practice. You may not notice any physiological responses prior to acting out with anger. But if you look closely, you'll see telltale signs.

COMMON PHYSIOLOGICAL RESPONSES TO ANGER AROUSAL

Muscle Tension. The body feels tense and vigilant. Many people experience tension in the neck, shoulders, back, or chest.

Increased Heart Rate. You may experience anything from a slight increase in your heart rate to feeling your heart pounding in your chest.

Rapid Breathing. Breathing becomes more rapid and shallow.

Perspiration. Some people experience their body "heating up." This may include perspiration from the face, neck, underarms, or hands.

Trembling. The release of adrenaline and noradrenaline into the body (which also causes muscle tension) may cause shaking or trembling.

Crying. Some people cry when they are very angry, either during an anger episode or afterward.

List your most common physiological responses to anger triggers in the order in which they occur (if possible). As you practice this skill, recognizing your responses will become easier.

First Reaction: _____

Second Reaction: _____

Third Reaction: _____

Fourth Reaction: _____

GAUGE THE INTENSITY OF YOUR ANGER REACTION

Before deciding on the best anger response, you must be able to assess the intensity of your anger reaction. If you feel overwhelmed by the physiological experience of anger, then you won't become cognitively or emotionally ready to engage in productive emotional discussions with others. You can think about the intensity of your anger using the following scale.

1. No anger at all. No physical agitation.

2. Slightly annoyed. Slight physical agitation.

3. Frustrated. More physical agitation.

4. Stirred up. Physical agitation still increasing.

5. Aggravated. Moderate level of physical agitation reached. Becomes difficult to hide physical symptoms.

6. Heated. More obvious external signals of anger.

7. Pissed off. More physical symptoms of anger. It's time to consider removing yourself from the situation.

8. Irate. More physical symptoms of anger. Less and less control. Remove self from situation.

9. Furious. Physically becoming overwhelmed by anger. Even less control of responses. Imperative to remove self from situation.

10. Ballistic. Full-blown physical agitation. Others may be frightened at this point.

Think about your last significant anger incident. What was the intensity of that experience?

_____

_____

When you think about a significant anger incident, try to recall how long your mood lasted.

_____ One to two minutes   _____ More than one hour

_____ About five minutes   _____ Half a day

_____ 10 to 20 minutes   _____ All day

_____ 30 minutes to one hour   _____ Longer than one day to one week

Cognitive Responses: The Power of Angry Thoughts

Haniya works extremely hard at her job. She was recently promoted to project manager in software development for a large, multinational robotics firm. Because she is valued for her organizational and technical skills, upper management thought she would be able to help her team meet important deadlines. There's only one problem: her team members. They come in late, hang around the break room drinking coffee, take long lunches, and give her dirty looks when she comes in the room. "Lazy incompetents!" she thinks as she looks at her coworkers. In team meetings, she finds herself pointing at coworkers and shouting incredulously, "What is your problem? Why didn't you get this done?" She feels that none of them can stand her and that's why they won't work hard. She often thinks, "Any project that involves these idiots will be a total disaster!" These thoughts keep her awake at night.

Our thoughts have a powerful effect on our emotions, our behavior, and how we perceive situations and people in our lives. We all have various "lenses" through which we view everyone and everything. These lenses are based on past experiences, perceptions, and preconceived notions. But sometimes these lenses can be quite inaccurate. Another way of defining these lenses is to call them *thinking distortions* or *thinking errors*. What's interesting about these distorted thoughts is that they are not necessarily true or real.

For example, I once lost my cell phone and became very angry, because I thought my younger child had hidden it so she could watch YouTube videos. I was convinced that this was the case. "This child always takes my cell phone, and now she's hidden it!" was the thought I repeated to myself. I continued to accuse my daughter of taking my phone, which she repeatedly denied. After a day or so, I found the cell phone at the back of the coat closet, where it had fallen out of my jacket pocket. Sheepishly I apologized to my daughter for wrongly blaming her.

Thoughts like that aren't real. Yet we often follow them, even when they can potentially cause us pain. Thinking distortions can increase our anger response by fueling our perceptions of how we are being thwarted in reaching our goals in a given situation. Below you'll find a list of common thinking distortions. Most people have a few default patterns among these and can recognize their influence in their thinking and behavior. See if you recognize any of them in your thinking.

Common Thinking Distortions that Can Increase Anger

ALL-OR-NOTHING/BLACK-OR-WHITE THINKING

Description: The other person is completely wrong in the situation, and I'm completely right. There's only one way to look at or behave in the situation, and I'm completely right.

Countering this distortion: Try to take in the other person's point of view. Put yourself in his or her shoes for a moment. How does the issue look from the other perspective?

BLAMING

Description: The other party or parties in the situation are responsible for your anger and your anger responses.

Countering this distortion: Try to stick with your own feelings and response. Ask yourself, "What am I not getting in this situation? What goals of mine are being blocked?"

CATASTROPHIZING

Description: The worst possible outcome will happen.

Countering this distortion: Ask yourself, "What are the chances that the worst-case scenario will occur? What are other possible outcomes?"

EMOTIONAL REASONING

Description: You think that whatever you feel about the situation is also the fact of the situation.

Countering this distortion: Ask yourself, "What are the facts of the situation?" Think about what has actually happened, and leave out judgments for the time being.

GENERALIZATION

Description: These things "always" happen to you; things "never" go your way.

Countering this distortion: Remind yourself that there have been times when things went well. Situations don't always have the same outcome. You and others do not always act in the same manner.

LABELING

Description: Someone else's actions or character can be reduced to a negative label, leading you to name-call or have derogatory thoughts about the person.

Countering this distortion: Leave out judgmental language and name-calling. Again, what are the facts of the situation, without any colorful emotional language?

MINIMIZING THE POSITIVE

Description: Things go wrong far more often than they go right with the person, situation, or overall relationship.

Countering this distortion: Acknowledge positive interactions with the person you are angry with and other times when similar situations have gone well.

MISATTRIBUTIONS

Description: You are a mind reader or think you know the motives and rationale for another person's behaviors.

Countering this distortion: Stick to the facts of the situation. What do you actually observe with your senses to be happening? Leave out interpretations or assumptions about the other person's thoughts or motives.

NEGATIVE FILTERING

Description: You believe there are only negative aspects of a situation and no chance of a positive outcome.

Countering this distortion: Leave the window of possibility open. You don't necessarily know how things will turn out. Expand the lens from which you look. Search for any positive alternatives to what is happening now.

"SHOULD" STATEMENTS

Description: You believe that people should act in a particular way or situations should have a particular outcome.

Countering this distortion: Remind yourself that "should" statements are subjective. How you think someone should act or think may not be how that person believes he or she should act or think.

Haniya has displayed numerous examples of negative thought patterns about her work life; for example:

All-or-Nothing/Black-or-White Thinking: She believes that her coworkers are completely wrong and she is completely right.

Generalizing: She thinks that her team always messes up and never meets deadlines.

Labeling: She calls her coworkers terrible names.

Minimizing the Positive: She does not think about the times when coworkers get things right.

Now list the negative thinking distortions *you* most frequently use.

_____

_____

_____

_____

Through her participation in the women's anger management group, Haniya has worked to challenge her negative thinking. For example:

Blaming: She tries to think, "I am this team's leader. I can't blame everything on other team members."

Labeling: She realizes it doesn't help to call people names, and doing so will get her in more trouble.

Minimizing the Positive: She makes note of when her team does a task well and shares that with the team.

Now list thoughts that will help challenge *your* negative thought distortions:

_____

_____

_____

_____

Emotions that Often Accompany Anger

After completing a yearlong halfway-house stay, random drug testing, numerous 12-step meetings, court hearings, and supervised visits with her children, Emily was convinced she had at last proven her sobriety and stability. In her mind, she would soon have unsupervised overnight weekend visits with her two children. However, her ex-husband managed to convince the court otherwise. A judge ruled that Emily would continue to have supervised visits with her children in a family service agency for another year. She was devastated. Emily felt she had worked so hard to achieve her sobriety and had earned back her connection with her children. When she went to her ex-husband's house and pounded on the door, demanding to see her children, she felt rage—but also sadness and desperation. She felt devalued, ignored, and rejected.

Beneath the energizing emotion of anger, there are often other, subtle feelings occurring simultaneously. Below is a list of emotions that commonly accompany anger. Can you identify which feelings most frequently occur along with your anger? Check the ones that are relevant to you.

_____ Sad	_____ Anxious	_____ Accused*
_____ Desperate	_____ Afraid	_____ Guilty*
_____ Powerless	_____ Lonely	_____ Devalued*
_____ Ashamed	_____ Stressed	_____ Untrustworthy*
_____ Frustrated	_____ Depressed	_____ Rejected*
_____ Embarrassed	_____ Ignored*	_____ Unlovable*
_____ Hopeless	_____ Unimportant	

Terms marked with an asterisk are from Steven Stosny, Treating Attachment Abuse *(1995).*

Think about your most recent significant anger incident. Using the choices listed above as a guide, try to recall what other feelings, in addition to anger, you felt. If you experienced a feeling that isn't listed above, feel free to write that down below.

_____

_____

_____

_____

Styles of Anger Expression

Most of us have a default way of expressing anger that comes naturally to us. The ways that we express anger are determined by social and cultural norms and expectations. They are patterns learned while growing up in our families of origin. Your own physiology in regard to your sensitivity to anger arousal is also a part of the equation. Over time, your method of expressing anger becomes reinforced by the outcomes of your interactions with others and the world. For example, if you're conflict avoidant and continually suppress your anger, you'll probably never get what you want because others don't know that you're angry or what you want from them.

There are a variety of terms and methods associated with how people express their anger. *Anger inward*, *anger outward*, and *anger control* are all methods of anger expression that are associated with long-term increase in cardiovascular disease. *Anger discuss*, mentioned in chapter 1, is the only method of expressing anger that has been correlated with better health outcomes in the long term.

ANGER INWARD

In this particular type of expression, anger is denied, ignored, or stifled, and simmers painfully within you. Others may not be aware that you're angry, and long-term outcomes may include cardiovascular problems.

INDIRECT ANGER EXPRESSION

Here, anger is expressed through passive retaliation, such as talking about people behind their backs. This doesn't change anything about the situation.

ANGER SYMPTOMS OR "SOMATIZATION" OF ANGER

You may experience your anger through physical suffering, such as headaches or stomachaches. Others may not be aware that you're angry, so the situation doesn't change. This may result in ongoing physical problems.

ANGER OUTWARD

Here, anger is expressed outwardly at others, physically or verbally. You may tend to blame others for your anger. The people closest to you may start to avoid you or feel afraid to be near you. In the long term, you may experience cardiovascular problems.

ANGER CONTROL

Although you are aware of seething anger within, you expend a great deal of energy in carefully monitoring yourself to keep from exploding or outwardly expressing anger. Others may not be aware that you're angry. This may produce long-term cardiovascular problems, and it doesn't change the situation.

ANGER DISCUSS

In anger discuss, you talk about anger in a manner that is toned down with a person willing to listen. This is the best mode of expression for both relationships and health.

As you think back on your most significant incidents of anger either in the recent past or over a long time, what can you notice about these incidents? How would you categorize your style of anger expression?

_____

_____

_____

_____

Has your method of expressing anger changed significantly over time? Please describe how it has changed and why you think it has changed. Has your way of expressing your anger been beneficial to you in some way? If so, how? If not, please note that as well.

_____

_____

_____

_____

Learned Anger Responses from the Environment and Family of Origin

As mentioned in chapter 1, anger responses are learned in the social environment in which you were raised. Researchers have identified that as early as one year of age, people develop a preferred style of expressing anger. This style is learned from watching how the important people in your life interact when angry with one another, including you. Examining the impact of what you learned about anger while growing up can be an eye-opening process.

BOBBI: ANGER OUTWARD

Bobbi, a single mother raising a six-year-old daughter, is mostly proud of how she cares for her child. But she also feels stuck. Bobbi tends to revert back to the patterns of anger expression that she witnessed in her family growing up.

"There were four of us kids, and the house was full of stress. My parents were always worried about money. My mother was either at work or at home frantically preparing meals or cleaning; people were always yelling and throwing things. Nobody ever discussed anything in a normal tone of voice. Now, I have no problems with anger at my job—I am like an angel! But at home is where all my stress comes out, about money, about my daughter's behavior, anything," she says.

BEATRICE: ANGER INWARD AND SOMATIZATION OF ANGER

In Beatrice's family, nobody expressed any feelings. If you did express a negative feeling, like anger, sadness, or worry, you got ignored—frozen out.

"My parents and siblings simply wouldn't respond. They would avoid or run away from the conversation. My parents drank quite a bit—martinis every night with dinner—and I think that was how they handled their feelings."

Now Beatrice feels that she and her wife have a similar dynamic in their relationship.

"It's like there's a 'no feelings allowed' rule for me. But my wife feels she can dictate to me how things are going to be and I am supposed to just follow along," she says. "She's brilliant and organized and, in the back of my mind, I feel she knows best, but sometimes I don't agree. I don't bother to say anything and try to pretend I'm not angry. But more and more these days, I am experiencing headaches and back pain."

What was your family's overall style of anger expression? Did it lean toward the "hot" end of the spectrum, the "cold" end of the spectrum, or somewhere in the middle? Take a few moments and write about what you believe you learned growing up about the expression of anger. Do you feel you have adopted that style of anger expression in your adult life?

_____

_____

_____

_____

Anger Triggers

Researchers have found that anger triggers for women most frequently appear to be relational: intimate partners, children, family members, friends, and close coworkers. Raising children, experiencing work pressures, feeling rushed for time, enduring economic hardship, and self-deprivation can all create a perfect storm of stress factors that can lead to irritability and anger.

Take a moment to examine your most recent significant anger episodes. Was it an event, person, or place that triggered the reaction?

_____

_____

_____

_____

Targets

Researchers have found that as with triggers, women tend to make those closest to them the targets of their anger—whether they were involved or not. This was found to be especially true at work and in non-egalitarian male–female partnerships, where the power differential makes it unwise or impossible to express anger directly to the person who triggered it. In those scenarios, women target the other people in their lives or their property. This includes breaking things or throwing objects at the recipients of their anger.

Please take a moment to examine your most recent significant anger episodes. Can you recall who or what triggered an incident and who or what became the target of your anger?

_____

_____

_____

_____

Chapter 2 Self-Evaluation

By now you've examined the physiological, cognitive, and emotional underpinnings of your anger. You've also explored your personal style of anger expression and how you may have learned that style in your upbringing. You've probably learned a lot about your anger. But as we come to the end of chapter 2, let's look for patterns in the inception and expression of your anger and where you might begin to make changes. Write your answers below.

When you examine your most recent significant anger incidents, do you notice any precipitating factors? Are there specific times of day when anger is more likely to arise? Can you find any correlations to being hungry or tired or pressed for time? Can you identify any emotional states or specific situations? Who are the people most likely to trigger your anger and in what situations?

Time of day _____

Day of week _____

Hungry _____

Tired _____

Pressed for time _____

Worried about money _____

Who was involved _____

What situations were involved _____

What/who were your specific triggers _____

What/who were your specific targets _____

We will now take all of the data you have collected about your anger and apply it.

3 Acting Differently on Your Anger

BY NOW, you should be more familiar with your physiological responses to anger triggers. This includes the thinking distortions that fuel your anger and the emotions that accompany it. You should be aware of your style of anger expression, how you learned it in your family of origin, and what are the triggers and targets of your anger. You've also uncovered any precipitating factors that seem to make your mind and body ripe for angry responses. It's now time to take this information and experiment with taking a different approach to how you express your anger.

Putting Out the Fire: Managing Your Physiological Responses to Anger

Remember Margaret, from chapter 1? She was surprised to identify the many signals that her body gave her prior to the incidents when she'd found herself slamming things around the house or yelling at her partner, Jane. Becoming aware of her body's physical signs of anger arousal opened a new door for Margaret, giving her hope that she could monitor and manage the symptoms of her anger before they became negative actions.

Mindfulness

One of the ways that you can start to monitor your body's reactions to anger arousal is to simply become mindful of your breath and your body.

A few weeks into my women's anger management group, we start each group session with a simple mindfulness exercise for five minutes or so. These exercises help us connect with our breathing. They allow us to tune in to our sensations, thoughts, and emotional states and to notice what is going on around us. You may already be aware of mindfulness as a concept or have a regular meditation practice. If so, keep it going. Or, you may be like Margaret, who told the group that she "never took a conscious breath" in her life before trying mindfulness.

There is no right or wrong way to practice mindfulness; there is only practice. You can do it anywhere. So sit, stand, lie down, or walk; all that matters is that you're comfortable when you begin. You can close your eyes if you'd like (be careful if you are walking). If closing your eyes is uncomfortable, simply pick a spot on the floor to focus on as you practice.

Here is a very simple mindfulness exercise for you to try right now. If you you're not used to paying attention to your breathing, simply observe any thoughts or feelings that come and go within you. Do this mindfulness practice for one to two minutes.

> "If your house is on fire, the most urgent thing to do is to go back and try to put out the fire, not to run after the person you believe to be the arsonist. . . . So when you are angry, if you continue to interact with or argue with the other person, if you try to punish her, you are acting exactly like someone who runs after the arsonist while everything goes up in flames." —Thich Nhat Hanh

Focus on your breathing. Follow each breath as it enters your nostrils, continues through your windpipe, and enters and expands your lungs. Follow the breath as it exits your body through your nostrils or your mouth. Try to breathe evenly and naturally.

Notice any thoughts that come into your mind. Don't judge your thoughts or try to do anything about them—simply let them pass by, as though they were clouds drifting across the sky.

Notice any feelings that you experience. Again, whatever you feel, don't judge or try to change it. Simply observe the feeling, allowing it to rise and move on.

Become aware of any sensations within your body. You can start at your head or your feet or someplace else. Just notice what is happening in your body. Do you any have pain or tension? Any numbness or tingling? Are you cold, hot, comfortable?

Now allow your awareness to focus outside of your body. What sounds do you hear? What is the sound farthest away outside that you can hear? What sounds do you hear in the room? What sounds can you notice within your body? Can you hear your breath as it enters and exits your body, or your heart beating?

End the exercise by returning your focus to your breathing. Follow the inhalation from the very beginning to the very end as you exhale. After several comfortable, natural breaths, gently bring your attention back to the room.

After completing this exercise, take a moment to briefly write about what you noticed during this experience. When might it be most likely for you to practice mindfulness here and there during your week?

_____

_____

_____

_____

_____

_____

When You Feel Your Anger Is Getting Out of Control

As you may recall from chapter 1, it's difficult to think clearly, using good judgment, if your sympathetic nervous system is overwhelmed with an emotion, such as anger. If you feel that the intensity of your anger doesn't allow you to choose your responses to a situation, rather than reacting without thinking, you must take a step back and first calm your body's physiological reactions. Only then can you act differently and more productively in your anger response. Being able to listen to your body and honor what it's telling you is a major achievement for any woman who's learning to manage her anger in a more effective way.

TIME-OUTS

Emily sat in her house the day after her court appearance feeling furious despair. Her ex-husband successfully obtained a restraining order for one year, barring her from contacting him or her children. Now, Emily felt she had nothing to lose, so she picked up her car keys and drove toward the family home again. Feeling righteous rage welling up within her, Emily intended to confront her ex and finally convince him how wrong he was to do this to her.

When you feel that your anger is getting out of control, taking a *time-out* is a crucial technique to help quell your emotions. This doesn't mean you're giving up or giving in; you'll still get that chance to have your say. A time-out is a moment, and some space, to cool down and collect your thoughts. It gives you a chance to make a reasoned response to an anger-provoking situation.

If Emily had given herself a few minutes to cool down before she got into her car and sped off to see her children, she would've had time to rethink her actions. Perhaps she would've realized that her actions would violate the restraining order and considered the dire consequences that violation would cause in terms of her relationship with her children.

To properly use the time-out technique, inform the person you feel anger toward that you're going to take a time-out and will be back when you've cooled down. If you find yourself in an escalating argument with a coworker, your boss, your partner, or your child, use a simple but clear statement.

"Things are getting too heated right now, so I am going to take a few minutes to calm down. Let's come back to this when we are both less angry." This kind of language is assertive enough to make your point but hits the right tone in terms of not escalating the situation any further.

Be sure to find a safe space and take at least 30 minutes to calm down. After we have experienced intense anger arousal, it takes this long for our parasympathetic nervous system to calm down.

TIPP SKILLS

TIPP stands for "tip the temperature, intense exercise, paced breathing, and paired muscle relaxation." The method comes from the Dialectical Behavioral Therapy (DBT) approach, devised by Marsha Linehan, PhD, to help individuals manage difficult emotions and harmful behaviors.

DBT was originally designed to help individuals struggling with the psychiatric diagnosis of borderline personality disorder, a condition that causes a person to suffer from overwhelmingly intense and fluctuating emotions, such as anger, depression, and anxiety; self-harming behavior; and dysfunctional relationships. Today, DBT skills are used for treating many other mental health conditions that involve intense emotions and dysfunctional behaviors. TIPP skills are useful as you learn to understand and work with your anger. In particular, they can help you refrain from acting on out-of-control feelings of anger. These necessary tools, which within the DBT framework fall under the category of *crisis survival skills*, make use of physical options for dealing with strong emotions.

As you learned in chapter 1, the intensity of your brain's physiological response to anger determines whether you will be able to use thought and judgment in choosing a response to anger, rather than reacting on pure emotion. These crisis survival skills are a series of physical choices you can make to help the body slow down its fight-or-flight response. They help the body lower the intensity of its physical reactions to an anger-provoking situation by changing body temperature or controlling breathing (and thus lowering heart rate) or by using intense exercise to help dissipate built-up energy from the anger response.

CAUTION: If you have heart or lung problems, allergies , or any other medical conditions that may affect your heart, breathing, or brain functions, please consult a medical professional before using these skills. The crisis survival skills change the body's chemistry, including lowering the heart rate. Some medical conditions may preclude using them, so please consult your doctor.

Tip the Temperature. This refers to using something cold in order to calm down quickly. When the feelings caused by intense anger begin to bubble up, you might try splashing or submerging your face in cold water or putting an ice pack on your eyes for at least 30 seconds. The cold water or ice pack triggers the body's *diving reflex*, which is its response to immersion in cold water. This automatic response triggers the heart rate and breathing to slow down, allowing the body to conserve energy and oxygen.

Intense Exercise. Provide a physical outlet for the energy that anger builds within the body. By engaging in vigorous exercise, even briefly, your body is able to discharge built-up energy. This practice releases endorphins, a pain-relieving hormone. Running, walking quickly, or doing jumping jacks or sit-ups can help bring relief to the agitation of anger.

Paced Breathing. Controlled, deep breathing is when the exhalation is generally longer than the inhalation and follows a brief period of holding the breath in between. Some people practice paced breathing by counting. For example, the 4-4-8 technique consists of breathing in for four counts, holding the breath for four counts, and breathing out for eight counts. You can use whatever intervals feel comfortable, but keep in mind that the exhalation should be longer than the inhalation and the holding count. Using paced breathing slows down your breath and your heart rate, bringing about relaxation.

Paired Muscle Relaxation. Combined with paced breathing, this involves tensing and releasing your various muscle groups to further stimulate the parasympathetic nervous system. While breathing in, slowly and deeply tense each muscle or muscle group within your body. As you breathe out in a long, slow exhalation, release the tension in the muscles. Notice what your body feels like before, during, and after tensing and releasing the muscles.

Managing Angry Thoughts

Below, we will use ideas from Cognitive Behavioral Affective Therapy (CBAT) devised by Ephrem Fernandez, PhD of the University of Texas at San Antonio. This method is particularly useful to work on managing, reducing, and reframing angry, distorted thoughts. Dr. Fernandez's anger treatment model utilizes a three-part approach: the prevention stage, which incorporates behavioral strategies; the intervention stage, which uses cognitive strategies (which we will be looking at in more detail below); and the postvention stage, which involves emotion- or affect-focused techniques to look at the other emotions that occur alongside or underneath your anger.

THOUGHT-STOPPING

After a long day in the busy law office where she works, Bobbi was plagued by recurring, angry thoughts. "Why do I have to manage everything on my own all the time? If I knew my ex was going to leave me, I never would have had a kid with him!" Driving home in heavy Boston traffic, similar thoughts repeated in Bobbi's mind. By the time she picked up her daughter at the after-school program, she was boiling over with resentment and could barely focus on anything but her anger.

The CBAT approach helps you stop the negative, repetitive cycle of unhelpful angry thoughts by replacing them with calming thoughts or phrases. Using this technique may help you lower anger arousal. By repeating a word or phrase that denotes the opposite of anger, for example, "Peace," "Love," "Let it go," "Be calm," or "This, too, shall pass," we can attempt to stop the negative cycle of thinking.

Take a moment to think about what words or phrases you might find calming when you begin to experience unhelpful, angry thoughts. Make a note of these below and give them a try.

_____

_____

_____

REAPPRAISAL

If thought-stopping is not effective in interrupting the negative cycle, you can move on to another method known as reappraisal. Your judgment of whether the person who has angered you has done so intentionally plays a crucial factor in how angry you become. If you're able to step back and rationally reconsider your automatic idea that what has happened was intentional, you're more likely to reduce your anger response. Additionally, if you're able to review the hurt you felt by someone's transgression, it's often less than you originally thought.

DISTRACTION

If angry thoughts remain painfully persistent after attempts to thought-stop or reappraise, you may try passive or active distraction techniques. You might choose to watch a movie, listen to music, or take a nap. At other times you might find taking a walk, going for a run, or having coffee with a friend to be more helpful in distracting and interrupting your angry thoughts.

Make a note below of what techniques you have found helpful in the past or ones that you would like to try in helping to distract from angry thoughts:

_____

_____

_____

Expressing Angry Feelings through Talking, Writing, Visual Arts, and Music

Beatrice came in for an individual session to discuss her feelings of anger in more depth. Through mindfulness exercises, exploration of the origins of her anger-inward style, and examination of her communication patterns with her wife, she had connected her headaches and digestive tract problems with buried anger. She brought in a picture that she had painted; it was of a closed door in a dark room. I asked her what was behind the door, and she explained that she was. She was behind the door, unseen and unheard, and no one knew that she was there. She was furious that she couldn't open the door and was just stuck there, alone, with her fury.

Additional ways of productively expressing and exploring anger can be through writing, creating visual art (as Beatrice did), or making music. What are some creative ways that you may find helpful in exploring your anger?

In an emotionally and physically safe environment, and with an interested listener, you can begin to explore your feelings of anger, where they come from, how they affect you, and what you would like to do about them and the relationships in which they arise. You might find such a listener in a friend, a therapist, or a member of the clergy. Talking about angry feelings can be a huge step in helping release them.

Think about a safe person or people with whom you can productively discuss your anger. Make a list of these people:

_____

_____

_____

_____

When the Flames Are Out but Embers Still Burn

Slow-burning, simmering anger can live on inside us, long after the initial anger-provoking event has passed. This can be especially true if you've been victimized or abused in some way and your power was taken from you. This kind of anger is better known as *resentment*, and it can cause angry thoughts to fester, sometimes for many years. Sometimes these thoughts can be about seeking revenge or wishing horrible things on the people who have wronged you. Even if you receive an apology or restitution, the resentment may still live on. What a person who has been grievously wronged chooses to do with her anger is, of course, deeply personal, but evaluating the pros and cons of having resentments may be helpful in furthering the healing process.

RESENTMENTS

Resentments are experiences that cause us to feel that we have suffered an injustice and leave us feeling chronically angry with regard to this experience. As in Beatrice's case, as described above, you may feel victimized and disappointed in these situations. You may have little or no communication with the person or people who are the objects of your resentment. You may want to get even or see harm come to the person who has inflicted this injustice on you. Resentment has an emotionally protective aspect in that it can keep us from feeling more vulnerable emotions, such as sadness, abandonment, grief, and loss. As we consider letting go of resentment, we face the prospect of experiencing these painful feelings. Often, as in the case of trauma survivors, we truly have been wronged, and our resentments are valid.

However, resentment can take up a lot of space in our minds. In various philosophical and religious traditions, there are prescribed ways to let go of resentments. Some people find relief by praying for those who have offended them. Some meditation traditions teach compassion for those who have offended us. In psychotherapy, some people write letters to the person who has wronged them, detailing the wrong that was done and its impact. We say all the things we would like to say in these letters. Sometimes the letters get sent and sometimes not. At times, it's enough to just write the letter. Other times, we may want to read it to a therapist, trusted friend or family member, or member of the clergy. Some people devise "letting-go" rituals, such as writing the resentment on a piece of paper and burning it in the sink or putting it in the back of the freezer, where it can "cool off." How or if you choose to release a resentment is up to you. The only requirement is that it's done in your own time, at your own pace, and in your own way.

> **"Those who are free of resentful thoughts surely find peace."** —Buddha

RELEASING RESENTMENT

Take a moment to think about a resentment you may be harboring. Answer the questions below to further explore this resentment.

Person, people, or situation that has caused the resentment:

_____

_____

_____

How have you been harmed specifically?

_____

_____

What feelings accompany the anger of this resentment?

_____

_____

What are the pros of releasing this resentment?

_____

_____

What are the cons of releasing this resentment?

_____

_____

FORGIVENESS

For one week in every session, the women's anger management group that I lead discusses forgiveness. We talk about whether forgiving is necessary to heal and how it can potentially release us from suffering or set us up to be victimized again.

"I will never forgive my ex-husband for keeping me from my children," Emily says to the group. "I don't want to, and I don't see any point in it. I am not religious, and I see nothing to be gained from it." Other group members validate her experience but express different points of view. "It is terrible to live with the guilt of how I have treated Jane in the past," Margaret says. "I wish I could forgive myself a little, if only to be less distracted when I am with her now."

Forgiveness involves voluntarily letting go of negative feelings toward someone who has caused you to suffer in some way. Some people point out that forgiveness doesn't mean forgetting what happened or excusing terrible behavior. Ultimately, when, how, or whether to forgive is a personal choice that can only be made by the person who suffered the harm.

What are your thoughts about forgiveness? Do you think it's necessary for healing and moving on from anger? Do you think the experience of anger can be reduced without forgiving? Are you struggling with this issue in relation to healing your anger?

_____

_____

_____

Chapter 3 Self-Evaluation

In this chapter you learned about ways to act differently on your anger. You read about mindfulness techniques to become more present in the here and now, and how to pay attention to what your body is telling you. You were also introduced to crisis techniques for when your anger is out of control, such as using time-outs and TIPP skills. We explored the CBAT techniques to manage angry thoughts and process angry feelings through talking, writing, and making art. Finally, we looked at resentments you might be holding and considered the merits of forgiveness as an option in helping let go of anger. Please take a moment now to write what information has been most helpful to you in this chapter and what techniques you plan to try moving forward.

_____

_____

_____

_____

_____

_____

_____

_____

_____

4 Restorative Communication, Part 1
Laying the Groundwork for Assertive Discussions

Beatrice sat across from her wife, Sarah, at a window table in the restaurant where they had had their first date. It was their tenth wedding anniversary. The flickering candlelight and the small centerpiece—a vase of pink roses—made everything seem more romantic. But Beatrice noticed none of these details; she was seething with anger and resentment. She looked at Sarah and thought how smug and self-satisfied she seemed. Sarah occasionally cast a brief smile in Beatrice's direction as she kept responding to texts on her phone from business associates. They were working on a deal that would make them as "rich as Trump!" But Beatrice couldn't care less. She was sick of Sarah's "big career" and her self-centeredness. "If I walked out right now, I bet she wouldn't even notice!" she thought angrily. She felt unheard, unseen, and unloved.

WHEN YOU SEEK connection, understanding, acceptance, and behavioral change from others, you can sometimes end up hurt and frustrated. Anger-fueled, unproductive arguments are often the result of failed efforts to communicate your wants, needs, and preferences. You end up feeling reluctant to get your point across, and your anger simply goes unexpressed. It eventually emerges but in indirect ways, usually at the wrong times and at the wrong people. On the other hand, denying your anger, or attempting to control any active external expression of it, creates inauthenticity and distance in relationships. It also prevents you from speaking your truth. *Restorative communication* is the best way to repair relationships at work, at home, and in your communities that have been damaged by inappropriate expression of anger or the avoidance of expressing anger at all.

Repairing or restoring communication isn't about achieving peaceful acquiescence among all parties. It involves the honest, direct, clear, and respectful expression of *your* wants, needs, and requests. It also requires the ability to listen non-defensively to the wants, needs, and requests of important people in your life. This path requires courage and perseverance. If done correctly, the results make for happier, closer, and better-functioning relationships.

Fortunately, there are many excellent relational communication teachers, two of whom are referenced in this book. Marshall Rosenberg was a clinical psychologist who developed the nonviolent method for communicating compassionately with others and solving problems peacefully.

John Gottman is a clinical psychologist who, together with his wife, Julie Gottman, founded the Gottman Institute, which conducts research and training on marital and family relationships.

Their proven techniques offer concrete skills to guide us in repairing and restoring communication in our relationships.

Assess Your Conflict Style

To get a better idea of your conflict style, take the brief quiz on page 57. With it you can discover whether your style of conflict is competitive, collaborative, compromising, avoidant, or accommodating.

CONFLICT STYLE QUESTIONNAIRE

For each of the statements below, please check either "T" (true) or "F" (false) depending on how consistently close it is to your actual behavior. As you go through the questions, think about the person or situation in which you find yourself in conflict most frequently.

1. I often prefer to let others take responsibility for solving a problem.
   ☐ T ☐ F

2. I would much prefer to let the other person win the argument than to have ongoing tension with the person.
   ☐ T ☐ F

3. I must have the last word in an argument.
   ☐ T ☐ F

4. I would rather spend time focusing on the things on which we agree rather than negotiating the things we disagree about.
   ☐ T ☐ F

5. I think compromise is the best way to go in any conflict.
   ☐ T ☐ F

6. It is important to deal with the concerns of everyone in the conflict.
   ☐ T ☐ F

7. First and foremost, it is necessary to pursue my own goals in a conflict.
   ☐ T ☐ F

8. Preserving the relationship is more important than any conflict.
   ☐ T ☐ F

9. If it seems easier, I will give up my own preferences in favor of the other person's.
   ☐ T ☐ F

10. Even if I am in conflict with someone, I always ask for that person's help in solving the problem.
    ☐ T ☐ F

→

11. I don't like tension and avoid it if at all possible.

☐ T ☐ F

12. I like winning arguments.

☐ T ☐ F

13. I postpone conflicts for as long as possible.

☐ T ☐ F

14. I will give up some points in an argument in order to gain others.

☐ T ☐ F

15. In an argument, I try to make sure all issues and concerns are on the table.

☐ T ☐ F

16. Differences are not always worth discussing.

☐ T ☐ F

17. I will make quite a bit of effort to get my way in an argument.

☐ T ☐ F

18. In order to preserve the relationship, I will soothe the other person's feelings in an argument.

☐ T ☐ F

19. I will give in on some issues if the other person will too.

☐ T ☐ F

20. I always see some middle ground in a conflict.

☐ T ☐ F

21. I always strive to get my points across in an argument.

☐ T ☐ F

22. I give my ideas, then hear the other person's in an argument.

☐ T ☐ F

23. I try to convince the other person to see the logic and benefits of my point of view.

☐ T ☐ F

24. I don't like hurting other people's feelings in a conflict.

☐ T   ☐ F

25. I immediately walk away when I see an argument coming.

☐ T   ☐ F

26. I try to find a fair combination of wins and losses for all sides.

☐ T   ☐ F

27. If there is an argument brewing, I make myself scarce.

☐ T   ☐ F

28. I appreciate direct discussion of the problem in a conflict.

☐ T   ☐ F

29. I try to find a happy medium between my position and the other person's in an argument.

☐ T   ☐ F

30. I feel that it is important for me to always assert my wishes.

☐ T   ☐ F

31. I am comfortable seeking to satisfy my wishes in a conflict.

☐ T   ☐ F

32. If the other person's point is really important to him or her, I usually give in.

☐ T   ☐ F

33. In an argument, I try to stay quiet so my feelings don't boil over.

☐ T   ☐ F

34. I pretty much assume at the start of an argument that I will have to give in on several things.

☐ T   ☐ F

35. I want everyone to leave an argument as content as possible.

☐ T   ☐ F

Now tally up your score. The group of questions in which you scored the most "T" answers will indicate your conflict style (at least with the person or situation you were thinking about).

Group 1: Avoidant (Lose-Lose Style of Conflict). If you answered "T" for questions 1, 11, 13, 16, 25, 27, 33.

Group 2: Accommodating (Lose-Lose Style of Conflict). If you answered "T" for questions 2, 4, 8, 9, 18, 24, 32.

Group 3: Compromising (No-Win, No-Lose Style of Conflict). If you answered "T" for questions 5, 14, 19, 20, 26, 29, 34.

Group 4: Collaborating (Win-Win Style of Conflict). If you answered "T" for questions 6, 10, 15, 22, 28, 31, 35.

Group 5: Competing (Win-Lose Style of Conflict). If you answered "T" for questions 3, 7, 12, 17, 21, 23, 30.

Adapted from the Thomas-Kilmann Conflict Mode Instrument

As you can see from the above descriptions, the avoidant and accommodating styles of conflict lead to a lose-lose situation for those involved. Avoiding a difficult conversation doesn't allow issues to be aired and resolved. Similarly, if one or both of the people in an argument give in too much—don't stay true to themselves—both sides lose, because the outcome is inauthentic. The compromise conflict style offers a no-win, no-lose situation and is more of a neutral outcome for all parties involved. Here, neither party wins or loses, and the issue isn't resolved. The collaborating style of conflict resolution offers a win-win for all sides involved. This is the ideal outcome but takes a great deal more effort and skill for everyone involved. Finally, there is the competing style, in which there is a clear winner and a clear loser in a conflict, resulting in a win-lose outcome.

Please take a moment to note what you learned about your style of conflict in that brief assessment. Did any of your answers surprise you? How do you feel about your indicated style of conflict? How can you apply a more productive conflict style in your next disagreement with someone?

_____

_____

Conditions Required for the Safe Expression of Emotion during a Conflict

If you're going to attempt a discussion that involves strong negative emotions, it's vital to learn how to do it in a productive manner. Certain basic conditions must be met before attempting such a discussion. Ask yourself the following questions before you're drawn into an emotional conflict. You should answer "yes" before you try to work through a problem with another person when emotions are running hot. If at any point the answer to these questions becomes "no," call a time-out and end the discussion for the time being. If possible, express willingness to resume the discussion when things are calmer.

1. Are you able to recognize what you are feeling and gauge the intensity of it? If yes, then proceed to question 2. If no, do not continue with the discussion.

2. Can you access the appropriate verbal skills to talk about your feelings, without swearing, shouting, or name-calling? If yes, then continue on. If no, do not continue with the discussion.

3. Do you firmly believe that you have the right to feel what you are feeling and to pursue what is right for you? If yes, then continue to question 4. If no, do not continue with the discussion.

4. Is it a safe environment—emotionally, psychologically, and physically—for you to talk about your feelings? If yes, then proceed to question 5. If no, do not continue with the discussion.

5. Is your discussion partner willing to listen to your emotions and work on the conflict with you? If yes, then proceed with the discussion. If no, table the discussion until conditions are right.

Essential Communication Skills

In general, basic communication skills can be used to enhance any conversation you find yourself in. They're particularly helpful to improve the outcome of difficult discussions. You may have heard about these skills in the past, especially in the context of assertiveness. This means when you act and speak assertively, you make your needs, wants, and preferences known in a way that doesn't hurt yourself or other people. Assertiveness involves specific communication skills that can be learned. It's good to practice these skills on a regular basis so that when you're in an argument, where emotions are high and it's difficult to think clearly, you can still access these skills.

TALKING

When you are the speaker in a conflicted discussion, use "I" statements to indicate that you are taking ownership of what you're saying and how you feel.

In the book *Difficult Conversations: How to Discuss What Matters Most*, the authors advise:

> **WHEN YOU HAVE THE FLOOR,** be clear, stay focused on the subject at hand, and stay in the moment. State the problem as you see it. Be specific and concise, using "I" and "I feel" statements. Express your needs, wants, and preferences in a clear, direct, and respectful manner. Don't bring up issues from the past that aren't relevant at the moment. Don't dominate the conversation; include the other person or people. Ask open-ended questions from time to time to ensure that they're following the conversation and understand what you're saying. Be sure to ask for their feedback.

> **IN A DIFFICULT CONVERSATION** your primary task is not to persuade, impress, trick, outwit, convert, or win over the other person. It's to express what you see, why you see it that way, how you feel, and maybe who you are. Self-knowledge and the belief that what you want to share is important will take you significantly further than eloquence and wit.

ACTIVE LISTENING

Listening with patience and respect to another person with whom you're having an argument can be extremely difficult. Hearing something about yourself that you don't necessarily like, without interjecting or rebutting, isn't easy. But listening in a non-defensive way is enormously helpful in reducing conflict and moving toward positive resolutions. Active listening allows you to paraphrase back what you think you heard the person say. This helps check your assumptions by asking if that is, in fact, what the person meant. Having good listening skills also means paying attention to the person's body language and posture, voice, tone, and the feelings underneath what the person is saying.

After their anniversary date, Beatrice decided to talk with her wife Sarah about her being on the phone and conducting business during their time together. Beatrice had discussed with other women in the group how she might start talking with Sarah about the monument of resentment she felt toward her. She decided to start with one specific issue: Sarah's constant use of her phone. Beatrice picked a Sunday morning, when both of them would be at home, without other commitments.

After breakfast, Beatrice asked if Sarah could sit and talk with her for a few minutes about something that was important. Sarah agreed, looking wary. They sat down in the living room, and Beatrice chose to sit across from Sarah. She had practiced sitting up tall and straight, and she didn't cross her arms but held them loosely in her lap. Sarah looked at her expectantly.

Beatrice: "Sarah, I would like to talk to you about something that's been on my mind and really came front and center for me when we were out at dinner for our anniversary."

Sarah: "Yeah, it wasn't easy to get that reservation . . . I had to call in a favor to get that exact table."

Beatrice noted that Sarah looked anxious.

Beatrice: "And I appreciated you doing that. But I didn't feel appreciated when you started texting and making business calls when we were at dinner."

Sarah: "I know, I know." *(She speaks defensively, her brows knitting, mouth pursing.)* "I tried to tell the team that I would be out of pocket for a couple of hours, but something urgent came up!"

Beatrice noticed the sensations of anger rising within herself—her heart beating more rapidly, her breathing becoming shallow. She wanted to shoot back that Sarah always makes other things more urgent than Beatrice. But she made an effort to retain her assertive body posture, retained a neutral expression on her face, and took some deep breaths.

Beatrice: "I know you are under a lot of pressure, but I am asking that when we are together, especially for something as special as our anniversary, we spend time talking to each other. We have been married 10 years; let's honor that. I felt that you didn't value our anniversary, or me, as you spent so much time on the phone. Before or after the date would have been fine."

Sarah: "Okay, I get it. I actually have been feeling really guilty about that. I knew it was wrong, but I didn't know what to do. I feel so pressured by the team, and I don't want to look like I'm slacking. Sometimes I don't know how to get them to back off."

Beatrice noticed Sarah looking at the floor and that her shoulders were tensing and her jaw clenching. Then she leaned toward her and put her hand on Sarah's hand.

Beatrice: "Maybe we could brainstorm together how to set some limits with the team. Who knows, it could benefit their relationships, too!"

Sarah managed a little chuckle and took hold of Beatrice's hand.

FACIAL EXPRESSIONS

One look is worth a thousand words, or so the saying goes. During an argument, to convey an attitude of respect for the other person or people involved requires the appropriate facial expressions.

The importance of facial expressions in the process of active listening and non-defensive speaking can't be underestimated. Sneering, scowling, smirking, or rolling your eyes while you speak or listen can escalate defensiveness in the other person and reduce his or her willingness to participate.

If you are initiating a potentially difficult conversation with someone, be aware of your facial expression. Try to maintain a neutral gaze. Avoid a tense jaw, and try not to frown.

As in the situation above, Beatrice made a conscious effort to keep her facial expression neutral, even when Sarah said something that angered her. By the same token, if someone is sneering or smirking, you can point out the effect his or her facial expression is having on your ability to communicate. For example, you might try saying, "I would like to share honestly with you how I am feeling, but you are smirking right now, and I don't feel you are taking me seriously."

BODY LANGUAGE

Maintain neutral posture, sit or stand upright without being rigid, and face the person you're speaking with. All of these techniques can help convey respect and engagement in the conversation. Maintain eye contact as is culturally appropriate. Distance is also important—too close can appear threatening, but too far away can convey disinterest or reluctance to engage. Convey an attitude of openness and non-defensiveness; don't cross your arms, and allow your hands and arms to remain loose. Try to drop your shoulders if you notice that they're raised up in a posture of defensiveness.

Some women who have gone through the anger management group express that in their families of origin, or in their culture, maintaining an assertive posture during a discussion or argument isn't something they learned or were encouraged to do. Some women have been actively discouraged from holding themselves in this way, because it wasn't considered ladylike or it comes across as masculine or "bitchy." However, holding your body in an attitude of non-defensive assertiveness is an extremely powerful statement that commands, and gives, respect. If this is difficult for you, practice it in front of a mirror or with safe people who support what you are trying to achieve.

PAYING ATTENTION TO UNDERLYING EMOTION

It's difficult to read the silent clues of what the other person is feeling—but isn't saying—in a challenging conversation. But it's important to practice this skill, because it can make the conversation more productive.

People employ a variety of clues to express their feelings during a difficult conversation. They roll their eyes in exasperation, tap their feet, or look away to show impatience. It's not always negative expression. Sometimes people nod their head in understanding or look sheepish to express embarrassment. These expressions all mean something about the conversation's impact on them.

Let's again look at the above example of Beatrice and Sarah. When Beatrice first told Sarah that she wanted to talk, she noted that Sarah looked anxious. That gave her a clue that Sarah knew that something was wrong. At the end of the discussion, Sarah admitted she didn't know how to get her coworkers to back off when she took time off from work. Beatrice noticed that her wife was stressed and tensed. She viewed this as an opportunity to reach out to her to figure out ways to set boundaries around her nonwork time.

Nonverbal cues are critical clues when you're in a difficult conversation. These include body language, voice tone, and word choice. These cues are really emotions behind other people's anger, which can include sadness, anxiety, loneliness, guilt, or shame. Asking gentle questions about their feelings can help them be less defensive.

SUBSTANCE USE AND CONFLICT

In an altered state, we can't accurately gauge our anger level. It lowers our inhibitions, making it harder for us to control anger responses. If you or the person you're in conflict with has been using any mood- or mind-altering substances, it's likely that the conversation will quickly get out of hand. Drinking alcohol increases levels of the hormone and neurotransmitter norepinephrine (also known as noradrenaline) in the body. You may recall from chapter 1 that norepinephrine is one of the key chemicals released in the body when anger arousal occurs. It also increases impulsivity and the level of excitement experienced by the brain and body. Adding alcohol to an angry brain, or vice versa, is a recipe for a volatile reaction.

Take a moment now to reflect on your strengths and challenges as a communicator. In general, what are your strengths? What are your challenges?

_____

_____

_____

Now think about your communication skills during an argument. What are your strengths? What are your challenges? What skills could benefit from improving?

_____

_____

_____

You may have noticed by now that most of the work needed to prepare for restorative conversations with the important people in our lives has more to do with ourselves, not the other person. As one woman in the anger management group jokingly noted, "Jeez, 80 percent of what we are learning has to do with our own feelings and behavior. I was hoping that we'd learn how to make other people act right!"

In the group, we continue to return to the idea that we can't make anyone change. The only thing we can control is our own behavior. The overall goal is to work toward changing our perspective and our thinking and feeling responses. In exploring restorative communication, so far we have looked at changing our own negative thoughts and perceptions. We've also focused on improving our ability to speak clearly, actively listen, and observe body language that is tied to emotions while engaging in difficult conversations. We will continue our conversation about restorative communication in the next chapter. This is where the rubber meets the road: learning to more effectively express our wants, needs, and requests for change to the important people in our lives.

Chapter 4 Self-Evaluation

In this chapter you learned about ways to restore and repair communication with important people in your life. You identified your conflict style and learned what it means for outcomes of your interactions. You learned about the conditions that must be in place before emotions can be safely discussed and the skills essential for positive communication. These include speaking and actively listening in a non-defensive way, maintaining assertive body language, and paying attention to the body language and underlying emotions of the other person. We will build on these ideas in the next chapter, where we'll practice asking for what we want and need and requesting change from others. Take a moment now to reflect on what was most valuable to you in this chapter.

_____

_____

_____

_____

_____

_____

_____

_____

_____

_____

5 Restorative Communication, Part 2

Asking for What You Need and Want, and Requesting Behavioral Change from Others

Haniya faces a very challenging conversation at work. She is now on a 90-day performance plan—the goal is to ensure that Haniya maintains the appropriate professionalism when communicating with her team. This means Haniya needs to curb her angry outbursts at work and refrain from name-calling and yelling. She and her team are weeks behind in delivering work to a major client. She needs to talk with a key team member, Tom, to find out why his part of the project is so late. In their last discussion, she had called Tom a "lazy incompetent," and he reported her to HR. The anger management group gave Haniya support with this difficult task and brainstormed ways she could have this conversation with Tom to produce a better outcome than her previous interaction with him.

CONTRARY TO what some business managers and employees may believe, negative emotions in the workplace must be addressed in any problem-solving conversation. According to *Difficult Conversations: How to Discuss What Matters Most*, addressing these negative feelings is crucial because "difficult conversations don't just involve feelings; they are at their very core about feelings."

In Haniya's situation, she must acknowledge Tom's feelings about her past treatment of him and give him space to speak about his feelings. She also must address her own anger and frustration at the delay in the project and his part in it.

The Four Steps of Nonviolent Communication

Nonviolent communication conceptualizes violence not only in terms of physical violence, but also through harmful ways of communication that occur in subtle, day-to-day, interpersonal interactions. Moralizing judgments, denial of your autonomy and free will, making demands, and thinking that you deserve specific outcomes all lead to disconnectedness and lack of empathy.

Marshall Rosenberg, PhD, a founder of The Center for Nonviolent Communication based in Albuquerque, New Mexico, created a four-step process for productive assertive communication. Rosenberg's model emphasizes the idea that an individual must first be compassionately connected with herself before she can act empathically with others. The four steps are as follows:

1. **Observing.** Verbalizing what is seen or heard factually and without judgment. For example, "When I see you come home late . . . ."

2. **Feeling.** Expressing how you feel about what you observe with "I feel" statements.

3. **Needing.** Stating the human need that isn't being fulfilled by the situation, such as "I need your attention when we are talking about something" or "I need your help with cleaning up the house."

4. **Requesting.** Making a request for behavioral change from the other person.

We will examine these steps as we see Haniya apply them in her difficult conversation with Tom.

Haniya and Tom's Discussion

Before the meeting, Haniya takes some time to check in with herself to know and acknowledge what she is feeling. She is anxious about meeting with Tom, given what happened during their last conversation. Haniya is worried that a negative outcome could jeopardize her job.

But she's also still angry that he hasn't adequately performed his job. Haniya takes steps to deescalate her emotions in order to prevent her body from going into fight-or-flight mode. She does this by using paced breathing, sitting mindfully in her chair, and simply noticing the details of her surroundings while paying close attention to her breath.

Haniya consciously acknowledges but doesn't pay attention to her negative thoughts. Instead, she focuses on positive, encouraging thoughts, like "Soon this will be over. I can do this; look at all I have accomplished in my life. Even if I were to lose this job, my friends and family will still love me."

Haniya continues to consciously breathe deeply and even repeats the word *calm* to herself as she breathes. She attempts to allow tension to leave her body and makes an effort to keep an open posture. Tom enters her office and sits down.

First, Haniya offers an apology for her part in the way their previous interaction went.

Haniya: "Tom, I know we have a lot to cover in this meeting, but I would like to start out by apologizing for the way I behaved in our last meeting. I should not have called you names and realize that was very unprofessional and hurtful on my part."

Tom: "I doubt you would be saying that if I hadn't gone to HR."

Haniya continues to consciously use paced breathing to keep tabs on her emotions.

Haniya: "Well, I hope that I would be, but I guess we can only go forward from here. I am sure that you were very hurt by my words, and I assume it will take time for me to show that I can behave professionally."

Tom: "At this time, I am not accepting your apology. Only time will tell if you are true to your word about changing."

Haniya: "Okay, I can understand your hesitation. As you said, I can only demonstrate change moving forward. Now let's move on to the subject we need to discuss, which is our late project for Apex."

Tom: "Okay."

Haniya now follows the Four Steps of Nonviolent Communication to address the productivity problem with Tom.

Observing. **Haniya:** "Tom, when I observe you not at your computer for long periods . . ."

Feeling. **Haniya:** ". . . I feel frustrated and worried that the project is not moving along. I am very concerned that we can't make important deadlines. This will cause problems for our entire team."

Tom: "Well, I am actually running around trying to talk to people who aren't returning my e-mails or voice messages about the project. Actually, it would be nice if you backed me up once in a while and helped me get the information I need."

Needing. **Haniya:** "I hear what you are saying, and I'd like to help. When the project is having problems and you are stuck, I need you to tell me so that I can figure out how to help. I need you to please communicate with me as soon as you know there is a problem, so I can help."

Tom: "I'll try, but a lot of times you are not at your desk, either."

Requesting. **Haniya:** "Okay. I would appreciate it if you would try to contact me by e-mail or phone as soon as you know there is a problem. I promise that I will make every effort to back you up."

Tom: "Okay, sounds fair."

At group the following week, there are high fives and hugs all around for the great work Haniya did in this difficult conversation.

Please think about and describe a situation where you might use the Four Steps of Nonviolent Communication to improve a relationship with someone in your life.

Who would the person be? What situation would you like to work toward improving? Outline the steps below.

Person, Relationship, Situation:

_____

_____

_____

_____

_____

_____

_____

_____

Observing Statement: _____

Feeling Statement: _____

Needing Statement: _____

Requesting Statement: _____

Restorative Communication with Intimate Partners, Close Friends, and Family Members

In group, Beatrice came to a big decision. She decided to initiate another discussion with her wife to tell her how unhappy she was in the marriage in general and to make requests for changes in their patterns of being together.

John Gottman, PhD, is a nationally known psychology professor and cofounder of the Gottman Institute, a research-based institute providing resources and workshops for couples and specialized training for counselors. For more than 40 years, he's studied couples, their communication patterns, and what works and doesn't work to improve their relationships. In his book *Why Marriages Succeed or Fail,* Gottman outlines four simple steps to improve communication in an intimate-partner relationship, especially during a conflict.

1. **Calm yourself.** Do not enter into a conversation if you are emotionally flooded. We explored in chapter 1 the physiological changes that occur in the brain and body when an anger-provoking incident occurs. Take note of the level of emotional and physical arousal you are experiencing in response to the anger trigger. Take steps to lower your reactivity to a manageable level (3 or below on the 1-to-10 anger scale; see Gauge the Intensity of Your Anger Reaction, pages 28 to 29) using the TIPP skills (see pages 45 to 46) or time-outs (see pages 44 to 45).

2. **Speak and listen non-defensively.** Simply listen respectfully without trying to rebut or interrupt the other person. This also means expressing admiration and appreciation for the other person in whatever ways possible.

3. **Validate each other and the relationship.** As hard as it may be, acknowledging how the other person feels during a difficult conversation can go a long way toward diluting animosity. Bringing up a mutually fond memory or joke, or expressing care or concern for the other person, can also help create positive connection, even in the midst of conflict.

4. **Overlearn: Practice, practice, practice.** Make an effort to repeat the three previous steps. Once you've practiced a number of times, you should begin to see some positive changes in your communication patterns right away. As with learning any new skill, it takes practice, practice, practice.

We can see how these four steps would be useful in any conversation with any close person in our lives, but let's see how they play out in Beatrice's discussion with her wife, Sarah.

Beatrice had asked Sarah to meet her after work one day at a quiet local pub to discuss some things about their relationship. Beatrice heard the surprise in Sarah's voice as she agreed to the request.

1. **Calm yourself.** Just as Haniya had done in preparation for her conversation with Tom, Beatrice takes measures to calm her emotions, thoughts, and body before going to meet Sarah. She practices these steps as she waits for Sarah, who is 25 minutes late, to arrive.

2. **Speak and listen non-defensively.** After feeling a measure of success in their previous discussion, Beatrice attempts to take on the larger issue of her general unhappiness in the marriage and the lack of equity. Beatrice says to Sarah what she had been rehearsing for weeks.

Beatrice: "Sarah, for some time now I have been feeling unhappy in our marriage. I often feel ignored by you and that you don't respect me as an equal."

Sarah: "Don't respect you? What do you mean? You are my wife; everything I do is for you! I work for *us*. To pay for *our* lifestyle . . . You know what our mortgage is, what the car payments are! You know that on your salary, you don't contribute much."

Beatrice is prepared for this defensiveness and continues with paced breathing. She stays focused on what she wants to say, despite feeling her anger rising.

3. **Validate each other and the relationship.** Beatrice wants the conversation to move forward and remain productive, so she uses Gottman's third step, validating the other person and the relationship, to keep her tone positive.

Beatrice: "And I truly appreciate all that you do and how hard you work for the money that you earn. But I feel that you don't respect me as a person. For example, my work—I am a teacher, and even though I don't make as much money as you, that doesn't mean my work isn't valuable."

Sarah: "Wow, I didn't realize what I was saying back there. I feel awful that you don't feel respected by me. I am so proud that you are a teacher. I tell people all the time."

Beatrice: "That's great you are telling other people." *(She smiles.)* "Now just tell *me* once in a while!"

Sarah: "I know this job is taking too much of my time, and the stress makes me act like a jerk sometimes. And I have felt you pulling back . . . I have felt ignored by you too. We don't have any fun times together lately."

Sarah naturally moves the discussion to ways in which the couple used to spend enjoyable time.

Sarah: "I do miss our trivia Tuesday nights; you are unbeatable. I was always so proud of the way you kicked butt in the government and science categories."

Beatrice: "And I enjoyed showing off a little bit."

4. **Overlearn: Practice, practice, practice.** This conversation turned out well. It opened a door to future conversations between the spouses, although not all of them went as well as this one. There were plenty of disagreements to be sorted out, but Beatrice and Sarah now had a template to follow to have productive arguments and discussions.

Let's look at another example of Gottman's four-step process in action. You might remember the example of Brittany and Kyle from chapter 1's description of Anger across Gender Lines (pages 14 to 15).

Eventually, Brittany and Kyle came close to divorcing and ended up in couples' therapy. Brittany had been confiding in her coworker David about her situation at home and how she felt overwhelmed by all the responsibilities of taking care of the family. David—a divorced father of two kids—started helping Brittany out here and there on the weekends, when Kyle wasn't around. Sometimes he would take her kids (along with his) to the park so she could clean the house, and they would all have lunch together. Or he'd grab her list on the way to Costco and pick up the things she needed.

Soon, Brittany and David had established a weekend routine based on mutual assistance. After a while, however, Kyle began to question this "mutual assistance" and became angry at David's involvement in his family's life. He called David and cursed him out, warning him not to "come around this family ever again—or else!" A serious argument ensued, with Brittany accusing Kyle of being an absentee father and husband, and telling him he should just leave altogether.

Kyle accused Brittany of being unfaithful. For many nights Kyle slept on the couch, and he and Brittany didn't speak. It was actually David who suggested to Brittany that she and Kyle seek marriage counseling. He did not want to be responsible for the breakup of their family. Brittany and Kyle sought out a marriage counselor, who used the Gottman method.

Counselor: "It seems that there may be concrete things that can be done to help this relationship. Why don't we try the Gottman strategy we've been talking about to have a conversation about one critical area of your marriage. Where should we start?"

Kyle: "I want to start by talking about Brittany's unfaithfulness. The minute my back was turned, she was off with another guy!"

Brittany: "I have told you a million times, it wasn't like that! David is my friend and a single dad—and I might as well be a single mom! We were helping each other."

1. **Calm yourself.** The counselor reminds both Brittany and Kyle to calm their bodies' emotional reactions to anger through deep breathing and silence for a couple of minutes.

2. **Speak and listen non-defensively.** The counselor reminds both Brittany and Kyle to quell their defensive reactions and really listen to what the other is saying. This is very difficult, but Brittany begins.

Brittany: "For all the times I have asked you to stay around on the weekend and help with the kids and you have gone off golfing, I have become more and more hurt and angry."

Kyle: "So you find another guy?!" (The counselor reminds him to speak non-defensively.) "Okay, I was very upset to see David coming around and taking my kids out and spending time with you."

Brittany: "David is a good friend and kind of in the same boat as me."

Kyle: "But he is divorced; you aren't—you have a husband."

Brittany takes a deep breath; she decides to take the risk to validate Kyle and the relationship, even though she is still furious.

Brittany: "Yes, I have a husband who I love and want to spend time with, but who isn't around on the weekend."

Kyle sits quietly. The counselor asks what he is thinking.

Kyle: "I know that Brittany is right. I just feel stressed out by my business, all the bills, the grind . . . I sometimes need to blow off steam. But I never thought I'd find another guy around."

Brittany: "As I have said, David and I have been helping each other out. It takes a lot to raise kids. There are a lot of chores involved. I am not sure why you don't see that."

Kyle: "Well, you know that my mom was a stay-at-home mom. She used to do everything around the house, and my dad just worked. Seemed like she loved all that stuff."

Brittany: "It's different. I work full-time *and* take care of the house and the kids."

Kyle: (*He sighs.*) "Yes. I wish I made a lot more money so it would be easier on us all. You wouldn't have to work."

Brittany: "You don't have to make more money. I like working! If you just helped out with more things, it would be much easier for everybody and we could spend more time together."

Kyle: "I do want to spend more fun time with you and the kids. I just don't want it all to be about work and chores."

The counselor asks if Brittany and Kyle can take a look at their daily schedules and make practical changes that would spread out the childcare and house duties more evenly. She warns that it won't be easy and that they will have to practice, practice, practice the above three skills as they continue to negotiate.

Take a moment and consider any relationships in your life that might benefit from Gottman's four simple rules. Can you imagine opening a difficult discussion with a loved one in a non-defensive way? How might you counter a partner's defensiveness with validation? What might you say to validate the other person and the relationship?

_____

_____

_____

Restorative Communication with Children

Bobbi wanted to find some way to talk with her daughter, Shania, about her angry outbursts. They usually occurred when the two first got home after a long day of work and school. In the few hours that remained before bedtime, Bobbi had to make dinner, Shania had to do homework, and then Bobbi had to make sure Shania took a bath. Bobbi found herself irritably racing through these chores, snapping at her daughter, who was also tired and cranky from a long day. Bobbi realized she felt like a victim, alone and unsupported in raising this child by herself.

With the help of the the women's anger management group, Bobbi decides that she wants to make a fresh start with her daughter and redesign their evenings together. She wants to be honest about her own behavior. Going forward, Bobbi wants to model for her daughter how to better manage difficult feelings.

She decides to apologize for the angry outbursts of the past. She wants to explain her anger in a way Shania can understand and to give her daughter space to express what it's like to be on the receiving end of those outbursts. She chooses a time that isn't during one of their high-stress moments but when they are more relaxed. Bobbi decides to talk with her daughter one Saturday while they are having ice cream.

Bobbi: "Shania, I would like to say that I am sorry for the way I get very angry sometimes when we come home in the evening. I just want you to know that it isn't your fault, and I am working to manage my anger better."

Shania: "Whose fault is it, then?"

Bobbi: "I guess it isn't anybody's, really. The stress builds up in me, like lava in a volcano, and then boom! I guess I explode."

Shania: "Yes, and it is very scary."

Bobbi: "I am sorry that I have scared you by being so angry."

Shania: "I don't like you being like that. You know, Mommy, you really need a time-out when you act like that."

Bobbi: "That is an excellent idea. I probably need a time-out *before* that happens. Yes, maybe when we come home in the evening I could take a little time-out while you watch TV for a little while. That way I can be calmer for the rest of the things we need to do."

Take a moment and consider relationships with any children or young adults in your life. Would you like to discuss anger and how to better manage anger with them? Think about brainstorming ways to reduce stress in the family household with the children in your life. How do you picture this conversation unfolding? What would you like to say?

_____

_____

_____

Chapter 5 Self-Evaluation

In this chapter you learned about ways to restore and repair communication with important people in your life. We identified conflict styles and learned what they mean for the outcomes of your interactions. We learned about the conditions that must be in place before emotions can be safely discussed, and we reviewed the skills essential for positive communication. We walked with Haniya through a difficult workplace conversation as she applied the Four Steps of Nonviolent Communication.

We also learned about John Gottman's four simple steps for improving relationships and saw Beatrice apply them in a conversation with her wife. Finally, we saw Bobbi apologize to her daughter for past angry outbursts and offer suggestions for making things less stressful in the future. Please take a moment now to write what information has been most helpful to you in this chapter and what techniques you plan to try moving forward.

_____

_____

_____

_____

_____

_____

_____

_____

_____

6 Maintaining Progress

THE WOMEN'S anger management group has been meeting for nearly three months, and the graduation date is in sight. Haniya, Emily, Margaret, Bobbi, Brittany, and Beatrice are all impressed and proud of themselves and one another for the progress they've made in managing their anger. Now they turn toward making an aftercare plan to maintain their progress. Each is worried about backsliding. Emily, in particular, with an ongoing court case, wants to have concrete strategies to help sustain her progress.

Quick Strategies for Preventing Future Fires

Reducing your reactivity to anger-provoking situations requires a holistic approach, involving body, mind, and spirit. That may sound like New Age gibberish, but like it or not, humans are physically, mentally, and emotionally tied to their parasympathetic and sympathetic nervous systems. Remember, we are hardwired with the fight-or-flight arousal and the body's corresponding calming system. So if you want to be less easily angered, you must take care of your whole self.

STRESS AND STRESS MANAGEMENT

Stress and anger go hand in hand. If you have chronic, unchecked stress, it's likely you also have a short fuse when it comes to anger. It also makes you more susceptible to a host of health issues, including cardiovascular problems, being overweight, and developing diabetes. Researchers tell us that it's not so much the actual amount of stress in our lives that counts but our *perception* of stressors. In real life, regardless of our perceived stressors, if we want to reduce our level of anger, we must reduce our stress levels.

AVOID TRIGGERS

This may be easier said than done, but take a moment to examine your daily routines, and look for opportunities to avoid or remove anger triggers from your day. Are you always late for work? Try getting up a little earlier so you can leave sooner and avoid traffic. Do you have a relative that you don't care for but run into at family functions? Try to avoid or limit your time with that person at the next party. What about the coworker you sit near who constantly rubs you the wrong way? Limit your interaction as much as possible; keep it cordial and professional but also brief.

MINDFULNESS, MEDITATION, AND RELAXATION PRACTICES

Numerous graduates of my women's anger management group have reported considerable benefits from adding time for meditation a few times a week. During the fifth week, we introduce the practice, and the group begins the session by engaging in a five-minute meditation. This includes paced breathing, visualization, or progressive muscle relaxation. Over time, a number of group members have discovered free and subscription-based applications downloadable to their phones that have made meditation even easier and more accessible.

Meditation doesn't have to be elaborate or tied to any religion or philosophy. It's merely a moment when you allow yourself to sit quietly, concentrate on your breathing, and practice letting go of certain thoughts and feelings.

QUIZ: PROTECTIVE FACTORS AGAINST STRESS

Protective factors are the positive people, activities, and personal care actions in your life that can help prevent certain stressors from happening in the first place or help reduce the negative impact of those that are inevitable.

Take this quiz to find out how many protective factors you have in your life against stress. Rate each item from 1 (*almost always*) to 5 (*never*) according to how often the statement is true in your life.

_____ **1.** I discuss my feelings when I am angry or worried.

_____ **2.** I don't smoke cigarettes.

_____ **3.** I get out regularly and socialize.

_____ **4.** My health is good.

_____ **5.** I get sufficient sleep for me to awake rested, at least four nights a week.

_____ **6.** I have opportunities to give and receive physical affection regularly.

_____ **7.** I eat at least one complete, healthy meal daily.

_____ **8.** I have some daily quiet "me time."

_____ **9.** I drink fewer than five alcoholic drinks weekly.

_____ **10.** I have fun at least once a week.

_____ **11.** My weight is proportional to my height.

_____ **12.** In my household, we regularly discuss shared domestic problems as they come up (e.g., bills, division of labor with chores).

_____ **13.** I participate in aerobic exercise for at least 20 minutes at least twice a week.

_____ **14.** I drink fewer than three caffeinated drinks daily.

_____ **15.** I am able to manage my time so that I am not usually rushed.

_____ **16.** I have a group of friends who I like to spend time with.

_____ **17.** I have religious or spiritual beliefs I find comfort in.

→

_____ **18.** I have a dependable relative within 50 miles.

_____ **19.** I earn enough money to cover my basic needs.

_____ **20.** I have at least one friend I can trust and share important things with.

TOTAL _____

To get your score, add up the figures and subtract 20. Any number over 30 indicates susceptibility to stressors. If your score is between 50 and 75, you have serious susceptibility to stress. Any number over 75 indicates extreme susceptibility to stress.

Some protective factors against stress are more fundamental than others. If you don't earn enough money to cover your basic needs, don't have secure housing or enough food, or have no family or friends you can count on, your stress level is going to be chronically high in a way that can be crippling.

Similarly, societal oppression creates a level of chronic, daily stress that underscores many basic activities of daily life. I have worked with many clients in these situations. Some have waited many months, even years, to obtain Social Security disability benefits when they have been unable to work. During that wait, they are often completely impoverished.

Other clients have become homeless and live in shelters while they wait for months and years for housing. Still others experience daily incidents of subtle racism. I founded a nonprofit community mental health practice, because I recognized that the meeting of these basic needs is the foundation of good mental health.

If you're in one of the above situations, how you manage your anger and your assertive expression of it is even more critical. Yelling at the person who handles payroll in your company because your check is late won't get you paid any faster. Cursing at the person who is handling your rental application because he or she is saying that your credit score is low won't help you get an apartment. It's unfair that in a country as wealthy as the United States, many people are living paycheck to paycheck and have little safety net. But unchecked anger at the interpersonal level is ineffective and won't help your individual cause.

Adapted from Outlook Associates of New England Stress Management Quiz

Remember that you're working on your anger management skills for your own benefit *and* for the people most important in your life. Seek out whatever resources are available in the area where you live.

Being impoverished, coupled with a lack of social and emotional support in your life, can seem insurmountable. There's no getting around the fact that working on solutions to these problems is lengthy, frustrating, and extremely emotionally difficult. But to act on angry feelings in inappropriate ways at the interpersonal level only makes your life harder.

Please take a moment to assess your protective factors against stress. Are you surprised by what you discovered? What are your strengths in the area of stress protection factors? What are the challenges for you and areas for growth?

_____

_____

_____

_____

_____

_____

_____

_____

_____

BODY/MIND INVENTORIES

Twelve-step programs utilize *personal inventories* as a way of taking stock of many aspects of a recovering person's life, both internally and externally. These are meant as tools to "clean house," so to speak—to clear out any lingering negative emotions, thoughts, or memories that might ambush the recovering person into using again. The tenth step of the program specifically discusses in detail taking a personal inventory, also known as a *spot-check inventory*, both in the moment and at the end of the day. A spot-check inventory requires only a brief pause from whatever you're doing. You can find many spot-check inventory resources available online, as well as a host of apps to download.

The practice of taking a personal inventory has existed in different philosophies, religions, and other systems of thought for thousands of years. From Confucius to Pythagoras to St. Francis Xavier, the practice of self-examination has been prescribed and lauded, though often ignored. It so happens that 12-step programs provide a handy reference to these practices in our times. Whatever you may think of the 12 steps, there is great wisdom in periodically taking inventories of ourselves—physically, emotionally, and mentally.

In relation to anger, doing this can help us stop our fight-or-flight system from becoming fully armed when we encounter an anger trigger. To do a spot-check inventory, simply stop whatever activity you're engaged in at the moment. Tune in to your breathing. Check your pulse. What are your thoughts and your feelings? What is going on inside? How is your physical state? Take some deep breaths and repeat a calming phrase, such as "I'm okay in this moment;" "This, too, shall pass;" or whatever works for you.

Here is a way you may conduct a spot-check inventory of yourself at any time:

1. Tune in to your breathing at different times during the day. Feel your stomach go through one or two breaths; notice the rise and fall of your body cavity. Be aware of what you are physically feeling in your body.

2. Become aware of your thoughts and feelings at these moments. Observe them without judging yourself. What are you thinking and feeling?

---

3. What connections can you make between what has occurred during this day, or previously, that may have caused these feelings and thoughts to arise?

_____

_____

_____

4. Are there any changes you would like to make to your thoughts and behaviors as you go on with your day?

_____

_____

_____

SOCIALIZING

In the women's anger management group that I facilitate, I've discovered that participants who had a friend or relative with whom to discuss their problems fared better in managing their anger and increasing their positive health outcomes. Spending time with friends and acquaintances whose company you enjoy can inoculate you against stress and anger.

You may think you don't have time to foster relationships. Maybe your friends are scattered all over the world. But it's a good investment of your time and effort, for both now and the future, to cultivate a reliable social circle.

ENGAGING IN PLEASANT ACTIVITIES

When you engage in activities that are calm and enjoyable, you directly influence and change your brain's chemistry. Calm, soothing activities increase your serotonin level, which protects you against stress, improves your sleep, and helps regulate your appetite. Serotonin also plays a role in increasing the amount of happiness you feel, as do dopamine, oxytocin, and endorphins. Activities that get your body moving are pleasurable and rewarding, and they increase the levels of these chemicals in your brain.

MINDFULNESS VERSUS MEDITATION

Mindfulness, meditation, and breathing and relaxation exercises can calm and focus us in any given moment. They help us find relief from thoughts and emotions associated with anger. Practiced regularly, these tools can help reduce stress and tension in our lives. Mindfulness and meditation are not necessarily the same thing, although there is overlap between the two concepts.

Mindfulness encourages you to focus on the present moment, using your senses. What you are looking at? A painting in the museum. What you are holding? A stone in your hand. What are you tasting? A tangy, sweet orange. What are you listening to? The sounds of children playing and cars driving by. Using mindfulness to fully dive into each of these experiences—the stone is heavy and cold; the painting has thick, saturated brushstrokes—helps ground you in the present and put a stop to distorted thinking.

Meditation involves many techniques to focus the attention, but it's specifically intended to cultivate the mind toward stillness and letting go—to release painful emotions, beliefs, and thoughts. Through meditation, you can work toward developing specific aspects of consciousness, such as compassion, love, and tolerance. Here is a short meditation for you to practice.

BREATHING IN PEACE: A MEDITATION EXERCISE FOR RELEASING TENSION

1. Set a timer with a pleasant-sounding ringer for two to five minutes or whatever time you are comfortable with. As you continue to practice such techniques, you will be able to sit longer.

2. Sit comfortably in a chair with your feet on the floor, posture comfortably upright.

3. Breathe deeply into your abdomen for four counts, and say to yourself, "Breathe in peace." Pause for four counts before you exhale.

4. Breathe out from your abdomen and say to yourself, "Breathe out tension," for approximately eight counts.

5. Use your inhalation as a moment to become aware of any tension in your body.

6. Use each exhalation as an opportunity to let go of any tension.

7. Use your imagination to picture the relaxation entering and the tension leaving. Some people imagine themselves surrounded by a peaceful, healing rainbow with a multitude of colors. In your mind, select a color that represents healing, and breathe in. When you breathe in this color, feel its healing qualities enter your body. As you begin to breathe out, picture whatever color best represents the tension leaving your body.

8. As you focus on your breathing, allow any thoughts or feelings that enter your mind and body to come and go. Some people imagine their thoughts as clouds floating by in the sky or as leaves blowing away in the wind.

9. If you find your mind wandering, patiently bring it back to your breathing. This may sometimes be hard to do, but that is okay. Mastering the technique of silencing your brain takes time.

Within the "emotional regulation" section of the DBT curriculum developed by Dr. Linehan resides a long list of activities that help distract you from difficult emotions. Engaging in these activities can protect you against stress and painful events. The idea is to visualize your life as a scale, similar to the "scales of justice." One side has negative events and emotions, and the other side has positive events and emotions. The goal is to keep the scale balanced, or even tipped in favor of positive events and feelings.

For websites that provide lists of pleasant activities you can engage in, consult the References section of this book or feel free to develop your own.

NUTRITION

As mentioned in the Protective Factors against Stress Quiz (pages 85 to 87), drinking more than five alcoholic drinks weekly and drinking more than three caffeinated beverages per day can have a negative impact on your mood and health. The quiz also pointed to the importance of eating at least one healthy, complete meal daily. The effects of food on our mood and mental health are well documented. If you have access to health insurance, discuss with your physician or nutritionist the effect your dietary habits can have on your mood. Try to avoid fast food; processed foods, including refined carbohydrates; and foods with high sugar and salt content and saturated fats. A diet of whole grains, lean meats, healthy fats, and fruits and vegetables can help you maintain optimum physical, mental, and emotional health.

EXERCISE/PHYSICAL ACTIVITY

This is the number one way women managed their stress and anger. The anger study participants cited a number of ways they got exercise, from walking to running to gardening. Just 20 to 30 minutes of aerobic exercise that moderately raises your heart rate, two or three times per week, can help reduce your anxiety level, improve your mood, and protect you from stress and irritability. If you have cardiovascular issues, first clear any exercise plan with your physician.

SEEKING PROFESSIONAL HELP

If you feel a need for one-to-one or group work to learn how to better manage your anger, seek out a mental health professional in your community. A licensed clinical social worker (LCSW), licensed professional counselor (LPC), marriage and family therapist (MFT), psychiatrist, or even some advanced-practice nurse practitioners can provide mental health services. Start by asking your primary care physician for a referral. If you have health insurance, call your provider's member services to ask about accessing your behavioral health benefits.

The federal government's Substance Abuse and Mental Health Services Administration (SAMHSA) provides a National Helpline, 1-800-662-HELP (4357), which is free, confidential, and open every day, all year. It's an information and referral service for individuals and family members seeking help for mental health and/ or substance use disorders. The SAMHSA website also provides an online treatment locator. For more information about this website, please see the References section of this book.

Your Personalized Self-Care Plan

Now that you've worked through the exercises in this book, my hope is that you'll continue to practice some of the skills to better manage your angry thoughts and feelings, and follow the steps toward positive communication. Take a moment to develop your own personalized care plan in order to maintain progress you've made in reducing your reactivity to anger. Check off the skills and practices you have found particularly helpful and would like to incorporate into your life.

_____ Thought-stopping (see pages 47 to 48)

_____ Examining and reframing distorted thoughts (see pages 30 to 33)

_____ Using TIPP skills (see pages 45 to 46)

_____ Monitoring physical signs of anger arousal (changes in breathing, heart rate, perspiration, etc.) (see page 27)

_____ Eating better (see page 92)

_____ Drinking less alcohol

_____ Consuming less caffeine

_____ Using Rosenberg's Four Steps of Nonviolent Communication
(see pages 70 to 73)

_____ Practicing mindfulness and meditation activities (see pages 42 to 43)

_____ Addressing trauma events from the past that may affect mood and
behavior today (see page 6)

_____ Getting regular physical exercise (see page 92)

_____ Engaging in at least one pleasant activity a day (see pages 89 and 92)

_____ Using Gottman's four simple steps to improve relationships
(see pages 74 to 80)

_____ Spending time with friends and acquaintances (see page 89)

_____ Taking quiet "me time" each day no matter how briefly (see page 85)

_____ Using "spot-check" inventories to calm down and see how I am
doing internally, as well as to identify what I am feeling and why
(see pages 88 to 89)

What other techniques and strategies would you like to include to help you
better manage anger? What practices and skills have you learned in this
book that you would like to integrate into your life?

_____

_____

_____

_____

_____

_____

WHAT TO DO IF RELATIONSHIPS DON'T IMPROVE

As we've highlighted throughout this book, individuals can control only their own behavior. You can seek change from other people, and you can learn how to request these changes. Many of us avoid conflict because we fear that standing our ground could mean the end of important relationships. This prospect can provoke anxiety, if not terror, for some. The ending of a long-term relationship can have very serious emotional and financial long-term impacts.

A rule of thumb in couples counseling is to try to make the relationship as good as it can be, then reassess the situation. Tools that help you better manage anger and express it more effectively may not save a relationship that has become unviable. But they *can* make it possible to have difficult conversations and work through painful decisions civilly. This can be especially important when children are involved.

Seeking out professional help in the form of a licensed MFT or another helping professional may be a good way to have difficult conversations in a safe place. In some cultures, it may be more appropriate to ask a trusted family member to sit in and help mediate. Still other people might be more comfortable consulting their pastor, rabbi, or another member of the clergy for assistance in solving conflicts.

A good alternative dispute resolution method is mediation, or a negotiation between two or more parties, facilitated by a neutral outside party.

If you do choose to end an important relationship, it is crucial to find support from others outside the relationship as you go through the process of separating. If you have supportive family and friends, reach out to them and share what is happening in your life. Spend time with them, in person and on the phone, connecting and getting their feedback and support.

If you don't have supportive family or friends, now is the time to put effort into developing supports. As down and angry as you may feel, try to find support groups or meet-ups in your area for people who are ending important relationships. Although in-person contact is best, online communities can be very helpful when you are going through these times of crisis.

Moving Forward

THE END OF women's anger management groups is always bittersweet. Members are certainly glad to have completed their 12 sessions. Usually there's some trepidation about moving forward without the support of the group. Members get satisfaction and strength from hearing one another's stories and how each member implements step-by-step changes in her life. Many become concerned about how progress will be maintained, or who will listen to them recount their struggles with anger or laugh out loud with them at the trials and errors along the way.

As you've seen demonstrated throughout this book, there are many advantages to reducing your reactions to anger. Developing the skills to more effectively express your needs, wants, and requests for behavioral change from other people puts you on the right path in many aspects of your life, including improved relationships and improved physical and emotional health for you. At the very least, learning to better manage your anger won't make things worse.

In my observations over the years, it's easier to act better than to feel better. That is, you may find that making changes to your outward anger behavior will be easier than changing the thoughts, feelings, and physical sensations behind it. We like to say in the anger management group that anger is like an iceberg. The behavior is only the tip that can be seen above the water. But as with the *Titanic*, it's what lies beneath the water that is more important. The *Titanic* sank because it ran into the giant part of the iceberg that was submerged. In the human psyche, what's submerged are the feelings, thoughts, and physical sensations that come before angry outbursts or inbursts.

Changing your outward anger is often a huge accomplishment in and of itself. Not yelling, cursing, and throwing things is a big step forward (and undoubtedly a relief for those around you). But to deny anger, internalize it, and misdirect it can be just as harmful to you and your relationships. If this is your method of dealing with angry feelings, be prepared, because eventually you'll end up blowing your top. For those of you with anger issues, it's inevitable that you must look at what is submerged in order to begin to make sense of your reactions. In order to make changes in your thinking and perceptions of situations, you must also explore your physical experience of anger and the other emotions that accompany it. Enough can't be said about becoming aware of the physical sensations and changes that first indicate anger arousal within you. That is where it all starts and where you must begin exploration.

The members of the anger management group have learned to use many of the skills that are taught in this book in the context of their own lives. And just as they have, it's up to you now to take these strategies and implement them in your own life in order to reduce anger reactivity and increase effective assertiveness. You'll be surprised that even the smallest step can make a big difference. For example, choosing during an argument to listen non-defensively, as best you can, to someone you're angry with can make a big difference. You'll feel pride in yourself and your effort. And when you see that it has worked, you'll want to do more.

Each day, try to take one small step toward better managing your anger. Try out the skills to become more effectively assertive: time-outs, validation, "I" statements, paced breathing—there are plenty of options to choose from. See what works for you. Some things will work better than others, but remember to keep trying.

The scholar, activist, and Buddhist teacher Thich Nhat Hanh equates anger with suffering and misery for the person who is experiencing it. He views any reduction in feelings of anger through mindfulness techniques as a reduction in suffering and misery. He writes, "When we are angry with others, we spread our suffering and misery. When others are angry with us, they spread their suffering and misery. By better managing anger, we find our way to peace."

Remember that you are not alone on this journey, and like you, many other women are trying, step by step, in their daily lives to better manage anger. I wish you many inner rewards for your strivings, and a happier life.

Blank Self-Evaluations and Worksheets

Anger Exploration Journal

Trigger event:

_____

Three Ws of event (whom you were with, when it happened, what happened):

_____

_____

_____

How intense was your anger on a 1 to 10 scale (10 being completely infuriated)? _____

What physical sensations did you feel (e.g., increased heart rate, perspiration, trembling, faster breathing)?

_____

_____

_____

What negative thoughts fueled your anger (e.g., my child is purposely trying to drive me crazy, the driver of that car is ruining my day)?

_____

_____

_____

What were your physical expressions of anger (e.g., crossing arms, pointing, yelling, swearing, throwing something)?

_____

_____

_____

What was the outcome of this situation (positive, negative, neutral)?

_____

_____

Where do you think you could have done something differently?

_____

_____

_____

Adapted from Outlook Associates of New England Anger Log

FADE

Please take a moment to sit down and imagine how life will be when you're better able to manage your anger. Close your eyes or focus on a spot on the floor. Allow yourself to imagine a time, perhaps a few months from now, when you don't let your anger get the best of you. Record your experience below.

Feel (Imagine how you will feel both physically and emotionally if you were to manage anger better):

_____

_____

Appear (Imagine how you may appear differently to others if you were to manage anger better):

_____

_____

Do (Imagine what you would do differently if you were to manage anger better):

_____

_____

Empower (Imagine what you would be empowered to do if you were to manage anger better):

_____

_____

Make note of the ways in which you want your anger to **FADE** in the future. Hang on to these goals for future reference.

_____

_____

_____

_____

Common Physiological Responses to Anger Arousal

Muscle Tension. The body feels tense and vigilant. Many people experience tension in the neck, shoulders, back, or chest.

Increased Heart Rate. You may experience anything from a slight increase in your heart rate to feeling your heart pounding in your chest.

Rapid Breathing. Breathing becomes more rapid and shallow.

Perspiration. Some people experience their body "heating up." This may include perspiration from the face, neck, underarms, or hands.

Trembling. The release of adrenaline and noradrenaline into the body (which also causes muscle tension) may cause shaking or trembling.

Crying. Some people cry when they are very angry, either during an anger episode or afterward.

List your most common physiological responses to anger triggers in the order in which they occur (if possible). As you practice this skill, recognizing your responses will become easier.

First Reaction: _____

Second Reaction: _____

Third Reaction: _____

Fourth Reaction: _____

Gauge the Intensity of Your Anger Reaction

Before deciding on the best anger response, you must to be able to assess the intensity of your anger reaction. If you feel overwhelmed by the physiological experience of anger, then you won't become cognitively or emotionally ready to engage in productive emotional discussions with others. You can think about the intensity of your anger using the following scale.

1. No anger at all. No physical agitation.

2. Slightly annoyed. Slight physical agitation.

3. Frustrated. More physical agitation.

4. Stirred up. Physical agitation still increasing.

5. Aggravated. Moderate level of physical agitation reached. Becomes difficult to hide physical symptoms.

6. Heated. More obvious external signals of anger.

7. Pissed off. More physical symptoms of anger. It's time to consider removing yourself from the situation.

8. Irate. More physical symptoms of anger. Less and less control. Remove self from situation.

9. Furious. Physically becoming overwhelmed by anger. Even less control of responses. Imperative to remove self from situation.

10. Ballistic. Full-blown physical agitation. Others may be frightened at this point.

Think about your last significant anger incident. What was the intensity of that experience?

_____

_____

When you think about a significant anger incident, try to recall how long your mood lasted.

_____ One to two minutes

_____ About five minutes

_____ 10 to 20 minutes

_____ 30 minutes to one hour

_____ More than one hour

_____ Half a day

_____ All day

_____ Longer than one day to one week

Anger Self-Assessment

The following is an anger self-assessment. It's meant to uncover the severity and frequency of your anger responses. This is not a formal diagnostic tool, but rather it is for informational purposes to help give some direction to your anger management work.

Please respond to the following statements and add up your total score. Circle 1 for *never*, 2 for *rarely*, 3 for *sometimes*, 4 for *frequently*, or 5 for *always*.

1.   I often feel physical pain, such as stomachaches or headaches, when I am angry.

   1   2   3   4   5

2.   I try to hide my anger from others.

   1   2   3   4   5

3.   When I am angry at someone, I will gossip about that person or try to sabotage him or her in some other way.

   1   2   3   4   5

4.   When I am angry, I take my frustration out on those closest to me, not the person with whom I am really angry.

   1   2   3   4   5

5.   I am irritated by small things.

   1   2   3   4   5

6.   I have a short fuse.

   1   2   3   4   5

7.   When I really feel angry, I want to hit someone.

   1   2   3   4   5

8.   When I get really angry, I want to break things.

   1   2   3   4   5

9.   I have obsessive thoughts that make me angry.

   1   2   3   4   5

10.   It really irritates me when people don't understand what I am trying to tell them.

   1   2   3   4   5

11. I blow my top at least once a week.

    1   **2**   **3**   **4**   **5**

12. My anger outbursts upset the people around me.

    1   **2**   **3**   **4**   **5**

13. I get really impatient when someone is driving too slowly in front of me.

    1   **2**   **3**   **4**   **5**

14. I get angry when people break the rules, such as when they have too many items in the express checkout lane at the supermarket.

    1   **2**   **3**   **4**   **5**

15. When people are rude around me, it makes me angry.

    1   **2**   **3**   **4**   **5**

16. I find myself frequently irritated by specific people in my life.

    1   **2**   **3**   **4**   **5**

17. I feel a lot of shame and guilt about my anger responses.

    1   **2**   **3**   **4**   **5**

18. I often feel a lot of muscle tension and stress.

    1   **2**   **3**   **4**   **5**

19. I yell or curse when I am angry.

    1   **2**   **3**   **4**   **5**

20. I get so angry I feel like a volcano ready to explode.

    1   **2**   **3**   **4**   **5**

21. I get frustrated quickly when machines or equipment don't work right.

    1   **2**   **3**   **4**   **5**

22. I hang on to anger against people and situations for a long time.

    1   **2**   **3**   **4**   **5**

23. I can't tolerate incompetent people. They make me angry.

    1   **2**   **3**   **4**   **5**

24. I think people are trying to get away with things they shouldn't.

    1   **2**   **3**   **4**   **5**

25. I have angry outbursts when family members don't do their share of the work at home.

    1   **2**   **3**   **4**   **5**

TOTAL _____

Score Key:

80–100   Your anger expression is likely getting you into serious trouble with others. It would probably be worthwhile to seek professional help in addition to working through this book.

60–80   You may need professional help, but you certainly need to work on controlling your anger in a deliberate manner.

50–60   You have plenty of room for improvement. Reading self-help books on anger control could be beneficial.

30–50   You're probably getting angry as often as most people. Monitor your episodes of anger outbursts and see if you can lower your score in a few months.

Below 30   Good job. You are likely managing your anger well.

Adapted from Outlook Associates of New England Anger Assessment

Releasing Resentment

Take a moment to think about a resentment you may be harboring. Answer the questions below to further explore this resentment:

Person, people, or situation that has caused the resentment:

_____

_____

How have you been harmed specifically?

_____

_____

_____

_____

What feelings accompany the anger of this resentment?

_____

_____

_____

_____

What are the pros of releasing this resentment?

_____

_____

_____

_____

What are the cons of releasing this resentment?

_____

_____

_____

_____

Conflict Style Questionnaire

For each of the statements below, please check either "T" (true) or "F" (false) depending on how consistently close it is to your actual behavior. As you go through the questions, think about the person or situation in which you find yourself in conflict most frequently.

1. I often prefer to let others take responsibility for solving a problem.
    ☐ T ☐ F

2. I would much prefer to let the other person win the argument than to have ongoing tension with the person.
    ☐ T ☐ F

3. I must have the last word in an argument.
    ☐ T ☐ F

4. I would rather spend time focusing on the things on which we agree rather than negotiating the things we disagree about.
    ☐ T ☐ F

5. I think compromise is the best way to go in any conflict.
    ☐ T ☐ F

6. It is important to deal with the concerns of everyone in the conflict.
    ☐ T ☐ F

7. First and foremost, it is necessary to pursue my own goals in a conflict.
    ☐ T ☐ F

8. Preserving the relationship is more important than any conflict.
    ☐ T ☐ F

9. If it seems easier, I will give up my own preferences in favor of the other person's.
    ☐ T ☐ F

10. Even if I am in conflict with someone, I always ask for that person's help in solving the problem.
    ☐ T ☐ F

11. I don't like tension and avoid it if at all possible.

☐ **T** ☐ **F**

12. I like winning arguments.

☐ **T** ☐ **F**

13. I postpone conflicts for as long as possible.

☐ **T** ☐ **F**

14. I will give up some points in an argument in order to gain others.

☐ **T** ☐ **F**

15. In an argument, I try to make sure all issues and concerns are on the table.

☐ **T** ☐ **F**

16. Differences are not always worth discussing.

☐ **T** ☐ **F**

17. I will make quite a bit of effort to get my way in an argument.

☐ **T** ☐ **F**

18. In order to preserve the relationship, I will soothe the other person's feelings in an argument.

☐ **T** ☐ **F**

19. I will give in on some issues if the other person will, too.

☐ **T** ☐ **F**

20. I always see some middle ground in a conflict.

☐ **T** ☐ **F**

21. I always strive to get my points across in an argument.

☐ **T** ☐ **F**

22. I give my ideas, then hear the other person's in an argument.

☐ **T** ☐ **F**

23. I try to convince the other person to see the logic and benefits of my point of view.

☐ **T** ☐ **F**

24. I don't like hurting other people's feelings in a conflict.
☐ T ☐ F

25. I immediately walk away when I see an argument coming.
☐ T ☐ F

26. I try to find a fair combination of wins and losses for all sides.
☐ T ☐ F

27. If there is an argument brewing, I make myself scarce.
☐ T ☐ F

28. I appreciate direct discussion of the problem in a conflict.
☐ T ☐ F

29. I try to find a happy medium between my position and the other person's in an argument.
☐ T ☐ F

30. I feel that it is important for me to always assert my wishes.
☐ T ☐ F

31. I am comfortable seeking to satisfy my wishes in a conflict.
☐ T ☐ F

32. If the other person's point is really important to him or her, I would probably give in.
☐ T ☐ F

33. In an argument, I try to stay quiet so my feelings don't boil over.
☐ T ☐ F

34. I pretty much assume at the start of an argument that I will have to give in on several things.
☐ T ☐ F

35. I want everyone to leave an argument as content as possible.
☐ T ☐ F

Now tally up your score. The group of questions in which you scored the most "T" answers will indicate your conflict style (at least with the person or situation you were thinking about).

Group 1: Avoidant (Lose-Lose Style of Conflict). If you answered "T" for questions 1, 11, 13, 16, 25, 27, 33.

Group 2: Accommodating (Lose-Lose Style of Conflict). If you answered "T" for questions 2, 4, 8, 9, 18, 24, 32.

Group 3: Compromising (No-Win, No-Lose Style of Conflict). If you answered "T" for questions 5, 14, 19, 20, 26, 29, 34.

Group 4: Collaborating (Win-Win Style of Conflict). If you answered "T" for questions 6, 10, 15, 22, 28, 31, 35.

Group 5: Competing (Win-Lose Style of Conflict). If you answered "T" for questions 3, 7, 12, 17, 21, 23, 30.

Adapted from the Thomas-Kilmann Conflict Mode Instrument

Spot-Check Inventory

Here is a way you may conduct a spot-check inventory of yourself at any time:

1. Tune in to your breathing at different times during the day. Feel your stomach go through one or two breaths; notice the rise and fall of your body cavity. Be aware of what you are physically feeling in your body.

    _____

    _____

    _____

2. Become aware of your thoughts and feelings at these moments. Observe them without judging yourself. What are you thinking and feeling?

    _____

    _____

    _____

3. What connections can you make between what has occurred during this day, or previously, that may have caused these feelings and thoughts to arise?

    _____

    _____

    _____

4. Are there any changes you would like to make to your thoughts and behaviors as you go on with your day?

    _____

    _____

    _____

Resources

HELPLINES

National Parent Helpline

Phone: 1-855-4APARENT (1-855-427-2736), available weekdays, 10 a.m. to 7 p.m. PST

This helpline serves parents and caregivers needing emotional support, and provides links to resources.

Alzheimer's Association

Phone: 1-800-272-3900, available every day, 24 hours a day

This helpline serves people with memory loss, caregivers, health care professionals, and the public.

National Domestic Violence Hotline

Phone: 1-800-799-SAFE (1-800-799-7233)

TTY (text teleIphone for deaf/hard of hearing): 1-800-787-3224

Videophone only for deaf callers: 1-206-518-9361

This hotline serves children, parents, friends, and offenders.

The US Substance Abuse and Mental Health Services Administration (SAMHSA) National Helpline

Phone: 1-800-662-HELP (1-800-662-4357), available every day, 24 hours a day

This is a free, confidential information and referral service for individuals and family members seeking help for mental health and/or substance use disorders. The SAMHSA website also provides an online treatment locator.

ONLINE RESOURCES

List of adult pleasant activities: https://www.dbtselfhelp.com/html/er_handout_8.html

Outlook Associates of New England, http://www.outlookassociates.com

Neighborhood Counseling and Community Services self-help pages and anger management worksheets found in this book, http://www.neighborhoodcounselingservices.org

BOOKS

Faber, Adele, and Elaine Mazlish. *How to Talk So Kids Will Listen and Listen So Kids Will Talk*. New York: Simon and Schuster, 1980.

Gottman, John M. *Why Marriages Succeed or Fail*. New York: Simon and Schuster, 1995.

Kassinove, Howard, and Raymond Chip Tafrate. *Anger Management: The Complete Treatment Guidebook for Practitioners*. Atascadero, CA: Impact Publishers, 2002.

Lerner, Harriet. *The Dance of Anger: A Woman's Guide to Changing the Patterns of Intimate Relationships*. New York: Harper & Row, 1985.

Linehan, Marsha M. *DBT Skills Training Manual*. 2nd ed. New York: Guilford Press, 2015.

Stone, Douglas, Bruce Patton, and Sheila Heen. *Difficult Conversations: How to Discuss What Matters Most*. 2nd ed. New York: Penguin Books, 2010.

Stosny, Steven. *Treating Attachment Abuse*. New York: Springer, 1995.

Thich Nhat Hanh. *Anger: Wisdom for Cooling the Flames*. New York: Riverhead Books, 2001.

References

American Psychological Association. "Anger." http://www.apa.org/topics/anger/.

Barnett, Rosalind C., and Grace K. Baruch. "Women's Involvement in Multiple Roles and Psychological Distress." *Journal of Personality and Social Psychology* 49, no. 1 (July 1985): 135–45. doi:10.1177/0192513X94015002005.

Centers for Disease Control and Prevention. (2017, August 23). "Women and Heart Disease Fact Sheet." Accessed January 3, 2018. https://www.cdc.gov/dhdsp/data_statistics/fact_sheets/fs_women_heart.htm.

Chaplin, Tara M., Pamela M. Cole, and Carolyn Zahn-Waxler. "Parental Socialization of Emotion Expression: Gender Differences and Relations to Child Adjustment." *Emotion* 5, no. 1 (March 2005): 80–88. doi:10.1037/1528-3542.5.1.80.

Denham, Gayle, and Kay Bultemeier. "Anger: Targets and Triggers." In *Women and Anger*, edited by Sandra P. Thomas, 68–90. New York: Springer, 1993.

DiGiuseppe, Raymond, and Raymond Chip Tafrate. "Anger Treatment for Adults: A Meta-analytic Review." *Clinical Psychology: Science and Practice* 10, no. 1 (March 2003): 70–84. doi:10.1093/clipsy.10.1.70.

Dittman, M. "Anger across the Gender Divide." *Monitor on Psychology* 34, no. 3 (March 2003). http://www.apa.org/monitor/mar03/angeracross.aspx.

Droppleman, Patricia G., and Dorothy Wilt. "Women, Depression, and Anger." In *Women and Anger*, edited by Sandra P. Thomas, 209–32. New York: Springer.

Fernandez, Ephrem. "Toward an Integrative Psychotherapy for Maladaptive Anger." In *International Handbook of Anger*, edited by Michael Potegal, Gerhard Stemmler, and Charles Spielberger, 499–513. New York: Springer Science + Business Media, 2010.

Fields, Becky, Karen Reesman, Carolyn Robinson, Angela Sims, Kelli Edwards, Belinda McCall, Blair Short, and Sandra P. Thomas. "Anger of African American Women in the South." *Issues in Mental Health Nursing* 19, no. 4 (1998): 353–73. doi:org/10.1080/016128498248980.

Fischer, Agneta, and Catharine Evers. "Anger in the Context of Gender." In *International Handbook of Anger*, edited by Michael Potegal, Gerhard Stemmler, and Charles Spielberger, 349–60. New York: Springer Science + Business Media, 2010.

Fischer, Agneta H., Patricia M. Rodriguez Mosquera, Annelies E. M. van Vianen, and Antony S. Manstead. "Gender and Culture Differences in Emotion." *Emotion* 4, no. 1 (March 2004): 87–94. doi:10.1037/1528-3542.4.1.87.

Haynes, Suzanne G., and Manning Feinleib. "Women, Work and Coronary Heart Disease: Prospective Findings from the Framingham Heart Study." *American Journal of Public Health*, 70 no. 2 (February 1980): 133–41.

Matsumoto, David, Seung Hee Yoo, and Joanne Chung. "The Expression of Anger across Cultures." In *International Handbook of Anger*, edited by Michael Potegal, Gerhard Stemmler, and Charles Spielberger, 125–37. New York: Springer Science + Business Media, 2010.

Mirowsky, John, and Ross, Catherine E. "Aging, Status, and Sense of Control (ASOC), 1995, 1998, 2001." Ann Arbor, MI: Inter-university Consortium for Political and Social Research (Distributor), 2005. doi:10.3886/ICPSR2 It03334.v.2

Modrcin-McCarthy, Mary Anne, and Jane Tollett. "Unhealthy, Unfit, and Too Angry to Care?" In *Women and Anger*, edited by Sandra P. Thomas, 154–69. New York: Springer, 1993.

Outlook Associates of New England. "The Impact of Diet on Anger." (2012, October/November). Accessed February 5, 2018. http://www.outlookassociates.com/newsletter/pdf/newsletter-201210.pdf.

PTSD United. "PTSD Statistics." Accessed January 20, 2018. http://www.ptsdunited.org/ptsd-statistics-2.

Radke-Yarrow, Marian, and Grazyna Kochanska. "Anger in Young Children." In *Psychological and Biological Approaches to Emotion*, edited by Nancy L. Stein, Bennett Leventhal, and Tom Trabasso, 297–310. Hillsdale, NJ: Lawrence Erlbaum, 1990.

Russell, Sheryl S., and Barbara Shirk. "Women's Anger and Eating." In *Women and Anger*, edited by Sandra P. Thomas, 170–85. New York: Springer, 1993.

Saylor, Margaret, and Gayle Denham. "Women's Anger and Self-Esteem." In *Women and Anger*, edited by Sandra P. Thomas, 91–111. New York: Springer, 1993.

Scherwitz, Larry, and Reiner Rugulies. "Life-Style and Hostility." In *Hostility, Coping, and Health*, edited by Howard S. Friedman, 78–98. Washington, DC: American Psychological Association, 1992.

Schieman, Scott. "The Sociological Study of Anger: Basic Social Patterns and Contexts." In *International Handbook of Anger*, edited by Michael Potegal, Gerhard Stemmler, and Charles Spielberger, 329–47. New York: Springer Science + Business Media, 2010.

Schultz, David, Angela Grodack, and Caroll E. Izard. "State and Trait Anger, Fear, and Social Information Processing." In *International Handbook of Anger*, edited by Michael Potegal, Gerhard Stemmler, and Charles Spielberger, 311–25. New York: Springer Science + Business Media, 2010.

Seabrook, Elizabeth G. "Women's Anger and Substance Use." In *Women and Anger*, edited by Sandra P. Thomas, 186–208. New York: Springer, 1993.

Smith, Tom W., Peter Marsden, Michael Hout, and Jibum Kim. "General Social Surveys, 1972-2014." Machine-readable data file. Storrs: Roper Center for Public Opinion Research, University of Connecticut (Distributor), 2015.

Smucker, Carol, June Martin, and Dorothy Wilt. "Values and Anger." In *Women and Anger*, edited by Sandra P. Thomas, 129–53. New York: Springer, 1993.

Spielberger, Charles D., G. Jacobs, S. Russell, and R. Crane. "Assessment of Anger: The State-Trait Anger Scale." In *Advances in Personality Assessment*, vol. 2, edited by James Butcher and Charles D. Spielberger, 161–89. Hillsdale, NJ: Lawrence Erlbaum, 1983.

Thomas, Kenneth W., and Ralph H. Kilmann. "Thomas-Kilmann Conflict Mode Instrument." Tuxedo, NY: Xicom, 1974.

Thomas, Sandra P. "Anger and Its Manifestations in Women." In *Women and Anger*, edited by Sandra P. Thomas, 40–67. New York: Springer, 1993.

—"Emotions and How They Develop." In *Women and Anger*, edited by Sandra P. Thomas, 20–39. New York: Springer, 1993.

—"Teaching Healthy Anger Management." *Perspectives in Psychiatric Care* 37, no. 2 (2001): 41–48.

—"Women's Anger, Aggression, and Violence." *Health Care for Women International* 26, no. 6 (2005): 504–22. doi:10.1080/07399330590962636.

Thomas, Sandra P., and Semiha Atakan. "Trait Anger, Anger Expression, Stress, and Health Status of American and Turkish Midlife Women." *Health Care for Women International* 14, no. 2 (1993): 129–43. doi:10.1080/07399339309516035.

Thomas, Sandra P., and Madge M. Donnellan. "Stress, Role Responsibilities, Social Support and Anger." In *Women and Anger*, edited by Sandra P. Thomas, 112–28. New York: Springer, 1993.

Thomas, Sandra P., and Robert L. Williams. "Perceived Stress, Trait Anger, Modes of Anger Expression, and Health Status of College Men and Women." *Nursing Research* 40, 5 (September 1991): 303–307.

US Department of Veterans Affairs, National Center for PTSD. "Anger and Trauma." Accessed January 7, 2018. https://www.ptsd.va.gov/public/problems/anger-and -trauma.asp.

Wilt, Dorothy. "Treatment of Anger." In *Women and Anger*, edited by Sandra P. Thomas, 233–57. New York: Springer, 1993.

Index

P

Parasympathetic nervous
  system, 9, 18–19, 45, 46, 83
Personal inventories, 88–89
Physical activity, 92
Physical health, 3
Physical symptoms, 36
Physiological responses
  to anger, 6–10
  assessing, 26–29, 103
  managing, 41–46
Post-traumatic stress disorder (PTSD), 19
Prefrontal cortex, 7
Protective factors, 85–87

R

Reappraisal, 48
Relationships
  effects of anger on, 4
  ending, 95
  restorative communication in, 74–80
  socializing, 89
  as triggers, 38–39
Relaxation, 84
Religion, 6
Resentment, 50–52, 109–110
Restorative communication (AARM)
  about, 56
  with children, 80–81
  communication skills, 62–67
  with intimate partners/close friends/family
    members, 74–80
  nonviolent communication, 70–73
  safe expression of emotions, 61
Rosenberg, Marshall, 56, 70

S

Safety, 7
Self-assessment, 11–13, 106–108
Self-care, 20, 83–93
  personalized plan, 93–94
Self-evaluations, 25, 40, 54, 68, 82
Self-examination, 88–89
"Should" statements, 32
Socialization, 89
Somatization of anger, 36, 38
Spot-check inventory, 88–89, 115
Stress, 9, 84
  protective factors against, 85–87
  vicarious, 14
Submissive emotions, 2
Substance use, 66, 93
Sympathetic nervous system, 8–9, 26, 44, 83

T

Talking, 62
Targets, 39
Therapeutics, 19–20
Thinking distortions, 30–33
Thought-stopping, 47–48
Time-outs, 44–45
TIPP skills, 45–46
Trait anger, 18–19
Trauma, 19
Triggers, 14, 38–39, 84

V

Venting, 3
Vicarious stressors, 14
Violations, 2

Acknowledgments

THE WRITING of this book has been serendipitous. I am thankful to Elizabeth Castoria at Callisto Media for giving me the opportunity to be this book's author. I would like to acknowledge my colleague Joe Pereira, MSW, LICSW, CAS, of Outlook Associates of New England, who has been working in the field of anger management for over 30 years and who first invited me to run the women's anger management group. It's Joe's excellent curriculum that guides the group, providing a dynamic psychoeducational experience.

I would like to thank my mother, who worked two jobs and raised two children by herself back in the 1970s, when it wasn't so common. I'd like to acknowledge all mothers everywhere, raising children on their own or in other situations that are not easy.

Similarly, I'd like to acknowledge all of the caregivers everywhere (most of whom are women) paid and unpaid: family members, home health aides, certified nursing assistants, and early childhood professionals. These women work in stressful, unseen, underpaid, and underappreciated roles caring for our elders, disabled community members, and children.

I am thankful to Rona Troderman-King, LICSW, who at various times has been a friend, mentor, clinical supervisor, and therapist. With her many years of broad experience in the field of clinical social work, she is able to give thoughtful feedback on any number of cases and situations that stump me.

Many thanks to Lyn Styczynski, PhD, and Len Greenberg, PhD, of the Family Institute for the excellent didactic family therapy trainings and supervision they provided to me and other clinicians over the years at the Family Center, Inc., in Somerville, Massachusetts.

Thank you to my editor, Nana K. Twumasi, at Callisto Media, for shaping this book into a tool to help women work on their anger. I would like to acknowledge Sandra Thomas, PhD, and her colleagues for their pioneering work in the study of the everyday anger of women.

The writing of this book wouldn't have been possible without the cooperation and support of my husband, Kristof, and our children, Karolina and Severyn. Many a weekend the family saw only the back of Mom, sitting on a chair, clacking away on the computer keyboard, writing this book.

And, finally, I would like to acknowledge the hard work and courage of all the women who have come through the women's anger management group to date. It has been a privilege and joy to work with all of you and to witness your brave steps toward change. I have learned so much from every group member, each one intelligent, insightful, wise, and humorous in her own way. And I look forward to learning more from those still to come.

About the Author

JULIE CATALANO, MSW, LICSW, is a licensed independent clinical social worker who has been a practicing psychotherapist for more than 20 years. She is a graduate of the Boston University School of Social Work. Prior to entering social work, Ms. Catalano was the editor of the *East Boston Community Newspaper* in East Boston, Massachusetts, and taught English in Poland for two years as part of the WorldTeach program. Ms. Catalano worked as a community mental health clinician for Catholic Charities in Lawrence, Massachusetts, and as a family therapist and outreach clinician for the Family Center, Inc. (now Parenting Journey) in Somerville, Massachusetts. Ms. Catalano is the director of Neighborhood Counseling and Community Services, Inc., a nonprofit community mental health group practice dedicated to keeping community mental health services accessible to all. She is a member of the National Association of Social Workers, Massachusetts Chapter. Ms. Catalano resides in Somerville, Massachusetts, with her husband, two children, and their dog, Fluffy. You can connect with Ms. Catalano and find more resources at www.NeighborhoodCounselingServices.org.

About the Foreword Author

DR. SANDRA P. THOMAS holds BS, MS, and PhD degrees in education (major: educational psychology), as well as an MSN (major: mental health nursing), all received from the University of Tennessee, Knoxville.

Dr. Thomas chairs the PhD program and teaches doctoral courses at the University of Tennessee, College of Nursing. She focuses on phenomenological approaches to teaching and research. She chairs a transdisciplinary phenomenology research group that meets weekly in the College of Nursing. Primary research foci are women's mental health issues and recovery from abuse.

Dr. Thomas has served as editor of *Issues in Mental Health Nursing* since 1997. Currently, she serves on the board of the International Society of Psychiatric-Mental Health Nurses Foundation and is a member of the Expert Panel on Violence of the American Academy of Nursing.

CPSIA information can be obtained
at www.ICGtesting.com
Printed in the USA
JSHW031618120920
7796JS00014B/2